JERSEY
TROOPERS

SERGEANT FIRST CLASS
JOHN E. O'ROURKE

JERSEY TROOPERS

SACRIFICE
AT THE ALTAR OF PUBLIC SERVICE

Charleston | London

THE
History
PRESS

Published by The History Press
Charleston, SC 29403
www.historypress.net

All images courtesy of the New Jersey State Police Museum unless otherwise noted.

First published 2010

Manufactured in the United States

ISBN 978.1.59629.978.8

Library of Congress Cataloging-in-Publication Data

O'Rourke, John, 1962-
Jersey troopers : sacrifice at the altar of public service / John O'Rourke.
p. cm.
ISBN 978-1-59629-978-8
1. New Jersey. Division of State Police--History. 2. Police--Mortality--New Jersey--Case
studies. 3. Traffic fatalities--New Jersey--Case studies. 4. Police--Violence against--New
Jersey--Case studies. I. Title.
HV8145.N5O76 2010
363.2092'2749--dc22
2010010750

Notice: The information in this book is true and complete to the best of our knowledge. It is offered without guarantee on the part of the author or The History Press. The author and The History Press disclaim all liability in connection with the use of this book.

CONTENTS

Contents

FOREWORD

The New Jersey State Police was established in 1921, primarily to provide police services in rural areas of the state. The person who is most credited with establishing the state police and having the biggest impact on its formation was the first colonel, H. Norman Schwarzkopf. Prior to his position in the state police, Schwarzkopf was a graduate of West Point, serving as an officer in the U.S. Army. His military background greatly influenced the manner in which the state police was established, putting into place the strict discipline and military bearing that the "Outfit" is known for. He planted and cultivated the seed that would eventually become an organization rich in tradition and established practices.

Two of the most familiar and recognized aspects of the state police are the triangular badge, only worn on the hat, and the sharp French blue uniform, both of which have remained virtually unchanged through the years. The hat that is always worn by the trooper is adorned with the triangular badge that has the seal of the state and the trooper's badge number. The coveted number runs sequentially and is only assigned once, never to be reused. Each corner of the badge is occupied with a star, the stars representing the core values of the state police: "Honor, Duty and Fidelity." The smart and crisp uniform worn by the road duty trooper, or "Road Dog," is similar to the uniform of the very first troopers who went out on patrol on motorcycle or horseback. Unlike other police agencies, the state police has chosen to maintain the traditional look instead of adopting a more tactical style that has become en vogue.

What has evolved over the years is the function of the state police. To meet the needs of the state, the agency has diversified into many specialties. Troopers today may have state-of-the-art equipment in their cars and stations, in step with the times, but some aspects of being a trooper still remain. Ask any trooper about his or her first station assignment and he or she (that also has changed) will probably recount coming an hour before his or her shift to clean the station and make the coffee for the squad. Or they may tell how the senior, more experienced troopers sometimes refer to them as "recruits," in spite of the fact that they graduated from the academy, until they prove worthy of the title of trooper.

Experiences such as these are what bring us together, forming the fraternity of the Jersey trooper within the state police. Retired or active, we all share this common experience. It is because of traditions such as these, passed down from generation to generation, that a strong sense of brotherhood exists within the organization. It sets the trooper and the state police apart from all police.

John O'Rourke is attempting to give you, the reader, insight into these brave men and the ultimate sacrifice that they paid. Most lost their lives in motor vehicle accidents; others suffered serious injury or illness that eventually caused their premature death, while others were murdered. No one death is more tragic than another; what is true is that some are more recognized and celebrated than others. The author wants to personalize these special individuals and remember each equally. At its conclusion, I can only hope that you come away recognizing that this organization has been fortunate to have had in its rolls special people of many different backgrounds but with one common purpose: to serve the citizens of the Garden State. Let us not forget those who wore the uniform before us and always remember those special troopers whose lives were tragically taken.

Trooper Eliecer Ayala #5555

ACKNOWLEDGEMENTS

I would like to thank the following people for their help for this volume: Mark Falzini (NJSP archivist); Thomas Cavallo; James Wurtz; James Principe; Ronald Perozzi; Hugo Stockburger; William Baldwin; George Rose; Deanna (In & Out Deli); Denise Zimmerman; Donna (Yenser) Dawes; Lieutenant Colonel Joseph Flynn; Lieutenant Colonel Lou Toronto; Barbara (Perry) Adams; Patricia and Eileen Walter; Ann McManus; Barbara (Dancy) Hubscher and her daughters Cathy and Carole; David Dancy; Debbie Lamonico; Helen Hartwiger; Peggie and James Wirth; Virgina Scotland; Douglas Scotland; Peggy Mallen; Maureen Gonzales; Patrick O'Dwyer; Jeffrey Oslislo; Robert Monacelli; Gerald Dellagicoma; Cynthia Hetherington; Theresa Deehan; Robert Hanley; Colleen Lupo; Spencer Hildebrand; Robert Vargus Sr. and Robert Vargus Jr.; Betty Beylon; Peter Ardito; Francis O'Brien Jr.; Keith O'Brien; Monsignor O'Donnell; Monsignor Shenrock; Walter Gawryla; James Conn; James Wirth; Margarete Wirth; Patricia (Walter) Debbie; Eileen Walter; Sandra (Welenc) Pennipede; Mary Ann Yuengling; Colonel Joseph "Rick" Funetes; Kevin Burke; Michael Permenter; Colonel Clinton Pagano and Catherine Hudak for telling me about The History Press.

I would also like to thank the New Jersey State Police, Former Troopers Association, the Survivors of the Triangle and all those public, county and state libraries too numerous to mention, which helped tremendously with my research.

For those who I have failed to list, please forgive my omission and know that each and every one of you who have helped—whether big or small—I am deeply grateful.

Special thanks go out to Eliecer "El" Ayala for his help in making this book possible. Lastly, I would like to thank my wife, Ann, and my two children, John and Joanna, for putting up with "my project" for all these years.

BLOOD POISONING

William H. Marshall #63

August 18 was a hot summer day in the year 1899, especially so in the city of Newark. The city and date are significant because it is there and then that William Henry Marshall was born. One of the three oldest cities in the United States, Newark was a leader in the industrial establishment. It had tremendous growth in manufacturing and success both in banking and insurance development. It was a time when William McKinley was president, Foster Voorhees was governor of New Jersey and the horse and buggy was the main mode of transportation.[1]

The new century was approaching, and Marshall's parents, William and Mary, were enjoying the fruits of their labor. The Marshalls, a surname dating back to English and Scottish descent, had eight children. They settled in Newark and sent their children through the public school system. It was not uncommon to have only a grammar school education, and William was no exception. Like most people at the time, William started working early in life. Little is known of Marshall's life from fourteen until eighteen.[2]

The United States' entry into World War I, in April 1917, provides us with insight into Marshall's life. On May 4, the young man enlisted in the army. Marshall received his basic training and was assigned to the Seventy-sixth Field Artillery and Cavalry. He saw his share of combat during the war. One battle in particular occurred in July 1918 near Paris, France. Corporal Marshall took part in this major campaign by the Marne River. Ironically, several other participants in this battle would also become New Jersey

William Henry Marshall #63.

troopers, most notably H. Norman Schwarzkopf, the organization's founder. The fighting lasted for three weeks and proved to be the last major offensive held by the Germans on the western front. Marshall's service ended with an honorable discharge with him being awarded the equivalent of a silver star.[3]

By the summer of 1919, the twenty-year-old war veteran was working for Westinghouse Electric. Westinghouse, a company on the verge of entering the broadcast business, had enormous opportunity for its employees. Marshall started as an armature winder. Even though Westinghouse was a thriving company, Marshall made a bold move, leaving for a job with Edison Electric as an inspector. He would make a similar move in September 1921 by leaving to join the state police.[4]

The State of New Jersey had been trying to organize a state police force since the beginning of 1914; it wasn't until March 1921 that the State Police Bill became reality and was passed into law. Three months later, Herbert Norman Schwarzkopf was appointed the superintendent with the responsibility of organizing the force. Sixteen hundred men applied to be troopers; among them was a young armature winder and former soldier from Newark.[5]

William Henry Marshall, along with 116 people, entered training on September 1, 1921. The training was reminiscent of the military boot camp that

Marshall in his army uniform.
Newspaper photo, Newark Star
Ledger.

Marshall had endured. Marshall did remarkably well, graduating with an overall physical average of eighty-seven. He also obtained marksmanship credentials.[6]

On December 1, eighty-one people stood with enthusiasm and pride as they were sworn in, becoming the first troopers for the State of New Jersey. Within the state police, once a badge is issued, it is never recirculated, and Marshall received badge #63.[7]

The state was divided into two troops, Troop A for the southern part and Troop B for the northern. Marshall was assigned to the latter. Interestingly, Marshall wrote on his state police application that he wanted to be a mounted horse trooper. Destiny placed him on a motorcycle.[8]

Much documentation exists of the first years of the state police; however, little is known of Marshall's career. He was a trooper for over two years, yet his file provides little insight into the man. Furthermore, little is captured on the accident that claimed his life. However, one document exists that provides insight into William Marshall's personality.[9]

On July 8, 1922, Captain Othel Baxter authored a letter requesting that Marshall receive disciplinary action. Baxter wrote that Marshall, with "blustering familiarity" and "without the slightest invitation," had stormed into his office right in the middle of a meeting. Baxter was with Trooper Hamilton #134, who, according to Baxter, was discussing "police plans." Marshall said, "Howdy-do Captain, how are you?…[Then] slouched on thru into the open where he had parked his motorcycle at odds to all other transportation." Baxter concluded his letter by writing, "His actions then and since his arrival is not a credit to the force." There is an interesting and somewhat questionable postscript: "9 P.M. Trooper Marshall nonchalantly meanders in and asks for the key to Ford to go to Trenton Junction to buy some cigarettes. Answer, No."[10]

This correspondence leads the reader to believe that Marshall was impolite and bad mannered. However, a closer examination reveals an interesting fact. Two years after this incident, Hamilton had risen to the rank of captain. Presumably, Marshall thought that Hamilton was receiving favor and was expressing his disapproval. This declaration is supported by Hamilton's quick ascension. Certainly, this incident shows that Marshall had a nonchalant demeanor and wasn't afraid to express himself.[11]

Marshall's tenure with the state police ended on a lonely stretch of highway in Red Bank, New Jersey, on Monday, December 10, 1923. Responding to a struck child call, Marshall's rear tire blew out, throwing him from his Harley Davidson. His injuries were minor, and he was brought to Monmouth Memorial Hospital in Long Branch, where he was expected to have a speedy recovery. Unfortunately, after two days with family at his side, a sudden "acute case of blood poisoning set in." At 3:00 p.m. on December 12, Marshall passed away. Poor sanitary conditions were likely the cause.[12]

At the time of his death, Marshall was stationed out of the Shrewsbury station and became the first in a long succession of troopers to die in the line of duty. The funeral service was held on December 15 at St. Peters Church in Belleville, New Jersey. He was twenty-four years old.[13]

MURDER AT CHIMNEY ROCK

Robert E. Coyle #238

Robert E. Coyle was the first New Jersey trooper murdered in the line of duty. Despite this fact, little is known of the man. Robert Coyle was born in the bustling, historic city of Philadelphia on May 31, 1898. Raised in Philly, Coyle was of Irish heritage, originating from the counties of either Donegal, Tyrone or North Connacht. The Coyles were Catholic and gave their son a parochial education. Young Robert graduated from St. Stephen's Grammar School in Philadelphia. As he grew, Coyle gained great physical ability. The world was at war, and Robert decided to enlist in the United States Army. He served three years during the World War, but nothing is known of his service other than that he was a private.[14]

After his discharge, Coyle worked as a chauffeur in Philadelphia. In the early twentieth century, a chauffeur was a prestigious job that came with a great deal of responsibility. State police records indicate that Coyle worked for two years with the Pennsylvania State Police; however, the Pennsylvania State Police couldn't confirm this.[15]

Robert Coyle was invited to attend the eighth state police class, along with Herman Gloor #240. Only two badge numbers apart, side by side, Coyle and Gloor sweated through weeks of difficult training. His experience driving through the busy streets of Philadelphia paid off for Coyle, as he proved to be an excellent driver.[16]

Robert Coyle #238.

On April 1, 1924, Bob Coyle was given badge #238. Bob Coyle's tour with the "outfit" would be brief, as the tragic day that would take his life was only eight months away.[17]

The increasing criminal activity attributed to Prohibition was rearing its ugly head all over the country, and New Jersey was no exception. The Roaring Twenties were a difficult time in America. The phrase, coined because of the cultural movements taking place, could also be used to illustrate the turbulent events taking place between law enforcement, rumrunners and gangsters. An illustration of this is that on the day Coyle was murdered, gangsters pulled an armed robbery in Bloomfield, New Jersey, and troopers in New York shot and killed a rumrunner.[18]

The last page in Coyle's life is marked Thursday, December 18, 1924. Troopers John Gregovesir and Robert Coyle were supervising a payroll transaction for the Bound Brook Crushed Stone Company, which was a major quarry nestled in the woods of Somerset County that employed a large portion of the local population. Gregovesir and Coyle were sent to assist with the payroll distribution. The manager of the company, Charles Higgins, went once a week to the local bank, picked up about $6,000 in payroll money and delivered it using Chimney Rock Road. One day, two suspicious men wearing long army overcoats stopped Higgins, identified themselves as troopers and promptly questioned him. Afterward, Higgins asked for police assistance and designed a plan that would involve the New Jersey State Police. The plan was simple: the superintendent of the company, William Haelig, would pick up the proceeds and bring them to Higgins's house, where Higgins, escorted by the troopers, would deliver the money using an alternate route. Haelig took the usual payroll route, serving as a decoy. Higgins's plot worked, protecting the money and foiling the robbery.[19]

Higgins, Gregovesir and Coyle arrived at the quarry, and the payroll was delivered without incident. Little did anyone know of the danger lurking on Chimney Rock Road, as Haelig was stopped near the quarry by two thugs posing as state troopers who inquired about the money.[20] Haelig returned to the quarry and told Gregovesir and Coyle what had happened, and the two raced down the long quarry driveway and turned onto Chimney Rock Road in pursuit of the bandits.[21]

Traveling down the winding road—known today as Thompson Road—the troopers spotted a man fitting the description. Unbeknownst to the troopers, they were speaking with Daniel Genese, a hardened criminal who was a consummate professional—calm, cool and collected. He made a career of robbing people. Gregovesir and Coyle also noticed another man standing up at Dr. Donahue Lane (today called Donahue Lane). The troopers thought it wise to question the two together and, according to Gregovesir, drove Genese up to the intersection. Whether the troopers searched the man isn't certain. What is certain is that Genese had a gun.[22]

Genese was put in the back seat. Coyle went to sit alongside him and was instantly met with Genese shouting, "Stick um up." When Bob Coyle looked up, a gun was in his face. Coyle pulled his weapon, and Genese shot Coyle in the face. The gun was loaded with blanks but burned Coyle's face, giving Genese the chance to grab the trooper's gun. Genese then shot Bob Coyle with his own weapon. Coyle fell mortally wounded. While this was transpiring, Gregovesir pulled his gun, but was slow in doing so, and the seasoned criminal grabbed it. A round rang out, missing both men. Within the small confines of an automobile, one trooper was dead and the other was fighting for his life.[23]

While Genese's partner, John Anderson, a petty criminal, was running to help, Genese won the struggle and took possession of Gregovesir's gun. Genese later said that he could have killed Gregovesir "but didn't want the blood of both of them on [his] hands."[24]

The state police had just marked the one-year anniversary of William Marshall's death and now was faced with another death. The state police would stop at nothing to find the culprits.[25]

The senseless murder of Coyle made troopers apprehensive, for the realities of the newly formed organization were settling in. Leads came in as local residents reported seeing two suspicious men a few days before the murder operating a red sports-type vehicle. Colonel Schwarzkopf, in an interview, "tolled off on his fingers…the reasons he believed" those committing the crime were "professionals of some experience." Schwarzkopf said the gun used was loaded with two blanks, "an old gunman's trick." The weapon was neatly and conveniently concealed but readily available. Schwarzkopf elaborated further: "The bandits had successfully palmed themselves off as state troopers while gathering information about the pay roll; that the bandit was case-hardened enough to shoot immediately without compunction when the occasion arose."[26]

The investigation followed like a Hollywood movie; there was a multistate manhunt, and police from all over took part in varying degrees. State Police Captain Robert Hamilton set up a command post at Pluckemin. Hamilton had risen through the ranks rapidly and, with about two years of tenure, was commanding Troop B.

The next day, the newspaper headline read: "Trooper Slain by Captive; One Death in Hunt." Local residents were asked to help in the search, and William Morton, a local auto mechanic from New Brunswick, volunteered and rode sidesaddle in Trooper Harry Linderman's motorcycle. Linderman and Morton had been out all night combing the area when they were met with an accident. The mechanic was catapulted to his death. Morton left behind a wife and a young daughter.[27]

Then, suddenly, there was a break in the case when a local taxicab driver said that he had driven two individuals over the past several weeks up to the Chimney Rock Road area. The taxi driver said that the men spoke of two brothers from Hudson County, one of whom was called "Rags Reilly."[28]

In his frenzy to escape, Genese had left his revolver at the crime scene, and the gun proved to be unique. There were only five hundred manufactured due to an infringement of patent.[29] The weapon Genese had left behind couldn't be traced back to its origins, but it was believed to have been shipped to Paterson, New Jersey, by the manufacturer. However, records showed that it was never received. Presumably, some shady employee had traded the weapon on the black market.[30]

With only three years in existence, the state police could not have fathomed that it would be challenged with managing a complex, coordinated criminal investigation with state and local authorities involving a murder of one of its own. Efforts were now being focused in Hudson County. In light of the complexity of the investigation, two seasoned Jersey City Police Department officers were called upon. Lieutenants Charles Wilson and Harry Walsh were brought on board and proved to be excellent cops, bringing the investigation to a successful conclusion.[31]

The handgun that Genese had left behind was processed for prints by the two-month-old State Police Fingerprint Bureau. "Rags Reilly" was found to be a convicted murderer doing a life term in prison. Investigators focused on Reilly's associates and thumbed through "25,000 photos along with Gregovesir." Genese's photo was easily identified by Gregovesir. How could he forget the man who had let him live? "He had a murderous look...I'll never forget it," Gregovesir remembered. Three other taxi drivers came forward saying they too had driven Genese up to the Chimney Rock Road area.[32]

Investigators discovered that the red car Genese and Anderson had used was in the hills near Stirling, New Jersey. Authorities learned that Genese and Anderson had stolen a blue coupe and abandoned it in a garage at 127 East Second Street in Plainfield about 3:30 p.m. on the afternoon of the murder. From there, they picked up the red sports car they had hidden in a different garage and proceeded up to Chimney Rock. In the weeks following the crime, the red sports car came to be called the "murder car."[33]

Lieutenants Wilson and Walsh followed Genese's trail by searching the vital statistics registry and discovered that Genese had applied for and obtained a marriage license in New York in 1923. The record indicated that he had married a woman named Florence Kleffer. Kleffer lived at 172 Hopkins Avenue in Jersey City. Upon checking the Hopkins address, detectives discovered that Florence's mother had remarried and her last name was now Berberich. This led them to East Sixth Street in Plainfield, New Jersey, where they posed as census takers. Under this guise, it was learned that Florence was living with her married sister, Mrs. Paldino, at Mount Horob, which was close to the crime scene.[34]

Troopers stood vigil, waiting out in the bitter February cold around the Paldino home. The discipline that Schwarzkopf had envisioned for his troopers was now evident in their actions. Troopers went without sleep, food and shelter and refused to abandon their posts. Every trooper involved wanted to be there when the cold-blooded killer showed up. The credo of honor, duty and fidelity was being adhered to.[35]

On the afternoon of Friday, February 8, Daniel Genese was spotted entering the Paldino home. Troopers apprehended Genese inside the residence, and the brutal killer turned out to be unarmed and gave up without a struggle.

The exhaustive manhunt was over. The very next day, John Anderson was arrested in Jersey City.[36] Genese was interrogated and confessed when he was told his prints were on the handgun he had left behind.[37]

For their hard work and effort, Lieutenants Wilson and Walsh were awarded the Distinguished Service Medal from the New Jersey State Police. Seven years later, the state police would once again call upon Harry Walsh's expertise to assist with the Lindbergh kidnapping.[38]

On December 15, 1925, less than a year after the murder, Daniel Genese was put to death via electrocution. He asserted to the last minute that he didn't get a fair trial. Prior to his execution, his wife, two children, mother, brother and sister visited him. Genese remained calm, composed and fearless up to his last breath. The killer bent down, said an act of contrition with two priests and then was strapped to the chair, where volts of electricity soared through his body. It took three soars of electricity to kill him. John Anderson escaped this fate by receiving a lesser sentence.

Robert E. Coyle's funeral took place on December 22, 1924, at St. Veronica's Church on Tiosa Street in Philadelphia. Bob Coyle was twenty-six years old.[39]

SHOOTING AT THE SPEAKEASY

Charles E. Ullrich #232

Fourteen months had passed since Trooper Bob Coyle was murdered, and in that time the state police was working hard to suppress the ills of Prohibition. The Eighteenth Amendment to the Constitution was enacted in response to crime being at an all-time high—crimes that were mistakenly attributed to the use of alcohol. Now, because of Prohibition, criminal groups were prospering and becoming more organized, in turn making the crime rate rise.[40]

Within the state police, Charles "Charley" Ullrich had been making a name for himself. Born on August 21, 1900, in Paterson, New Jersey, to Frederick and Susan, Charles was one of four children; Susan, William and Arthur were his siblings. They were raised in a city known for its great waterfalls and textile manufacturing. The year Ullrich was born, Paterson was the leading manufacturer of silk and was called "Silk City."[41]

As a child, Ullrich didn't live far from the Passaic River. Presumably, he went to the great falls to see the mist rise up to cool the hot summer air and swam in the crystal clear waters of the river. The Ullrich children attended the local Paterson school.[42] After grammar school, Ullrich attended high school for two years. Why Ullrich didn't complete high school isn't certain. Regardless, two years of high school gave him an edge over most.[43]

In 1919, a year after the World War had ended, Ullrich entered the navy. As a sailor, Ullrich learned the activities associated with deck handling, deck maintenance, rigging and small boat operations. He rose to the rank of

Charles Ullrich #232.

boatswain's mate, where he was considered a master of seamanship. Ullrich concluded his military service in January 1923, at the age of twenty-two.[44]

The former sailor realized that he wanted to be a state trooper and applied. In the state police's short tenure, it had developed a reputation for being top notch. The troopers were viewed as intimidating and serious in their deportment, but always professional, and residents were embracing the state police and the need for such a trained and professional law enforcement entity.[45]

In the academy, Ullrich met Joseph A. Smith from Connecticut. The two men were young and had much to look forward to; they were embarking on a challenging and exciting profession.[46] On September 1, 1923, Charles Ullrich (badge #232) and Joseph Smith (badge #231) began their state police journey as graduating members of the seventh class.[47]

Shortly after becoming a trooper, Charles Ullrich was working with Trooper Daniel Dunn #34, who introduced him to a woman named Ruby Bonner. Bonner was Dunn's sister-in-law, and Ullrich fell head over heels for her. Before long, they were planning their wedding. State police rules required permission from the colonel to wed. Ullrich, having only been a trooper for a short time, didn't want to run the risk of being denied, so the two wed in a secret ceremony in Elkton, Maryland, in March 1925.[48]

Prohibition made the onset of speakeasies very popular. Most were formed or established by organized crime. Speakeasies were problematic not only for the crime associated with them but also because of the health issues relating to sexually transmitted diseases, as prostitution was also common at such places of business. The phrase "speakeasy" is derived from a person ordering an alcoholic drink and being reminded by the bartender to "speak easy" so as not to be heard. Police corruption was at an all-time high, and most local law enforcement officers were given their positions because of cronyism, nepotism or political favor. As such, many lacked integrity, and speakeasies capitalized by paying off the local law. Interestingly, local police corruption was an element that gave rise to the concept of a state police agency.[49]

In Passaic County, officials had a serious problem with houses of ill repute, which led the prosecutor, J. Willard Deyoe, to take action. Deyoe had been trying to rid the county of speakeasies for a long time. One such establishment was the French Hill Inn located in the township of Wayne. Deyoe implored Wayne officials to address the problem.[50] For one reason or the other, Wayne officials failed to meet Deyoe's request, leaving him with no other recourse but to turn to the state police. State troopers had helped authorities with similar problems in Bergen County. The state police vigorously subscribed to Schwarzkopf's command of pursuing and apprehending offenders as set forth in his first "General Order." Known as the "get your man doctrine," this order contributed to the success and popularity of the organization.[51]

Located on the outskirts of Wayne, the French Hill Inn sat back off the road, with many trees providing ample privacy to those patronizing the establishment.[52]

On the evening of February 17, 1926, Lieutenant D. Rogers #79, of Morristown Headquarters, sent two troopers to gather information for a future raid; this was to be an intelligence-only operation. Rogers picked two of his best troopers, Charles Ullrich and Matthew McManus #144. The square-jawed McManus had recently returned to work after an on-duty injury nearly claimed his life. He was a perfect match for Ullrich; both were tough lawmen who enjoyed the excitement and danger of police work. Interestingly, a week prior, Ullrich's mother had told her son that she was concerned for his safety because he was "making enemies." The Jersey trooper told her that it was "the life that he liked and that he intended to die with his boots on." Dreadful words for a mother to hear.[53]

Ullrich and McManus set off in a taxicab to the notorious inn. As they approached the inn, there was a steady snowfall. They arrived at midnight and were met by a guard. The inn had an elaborate setup with a locked iron

The French Hill Inn. *Courtesy of Robert Monacelli.*

fence, guardhouse, lookout tower, escape routes, secret hiding locations and a screening process to enter. The large man who stood at the gate was handed some money, and Ullrich and McManus were allowed in. Driving up the one-hundred-foot driveway, the men stepped out in front of the three-story stucco building. With smoke bellowing from the chimney, lights flickering in the windows and snow draping the area, it was a beautiful wintery scene—a scene that betrayed the actual events taking place inside. The two men with long overcoats walked in.[54]

Matthew McManus.

The place was set up with tables, chairs and a bar. It was a dark, dreary-looking place with the smell of booze permeating the air. Through the thick cigarette smoke, alcohol bottles could be seen lining the shelves. Wiping off the snow, the two troopers walked past the patrons scattered throughout the place. The troopers proceeded upstairs to the second floor, where they entered a small corridor and saw a sign that read "Private Dining Room." Continuing on, they entered a larger room with a staircase rising to a third floor. Only eight patrons were in the room, so the two undercover troopers sat at a table.[55]

The two watched the shady activities and the pretty women walking around, such as Anna "Dolly" LaPorte, Florence Anderson and Jean "Babe" Lee. Ullrich and McManus sat and watched one of them making lewd gestures while she danced, while the other women sat on the laps of men. Laughter and piano music filled the air, and when the time was right, willing patrons were escorted to private rooms on the third floor. The proprietor of the inn, Samuel Alessi, was serving a combination platter of booze, women and rooms.[56]

At some point, McManus went upstairs with Flo Anderson, an attractive twenty-two- or twenty-three-year-old with a nice figure, reddish brown eyes and short black hair. Flo's occupation was evident in her sartorial splendor; she sported a sleazy sheer garment, black pump heels, artificial eyelashes, bright painted lipstick and a face covered in makeup. Apparently, McManus's questions to her caused Flo to believe that he was a cop, and she stormed out of the room, leaving McManus to return to Ullrich.[57]

About 2:30 a.m., Ullrich and McManus observed Flo walk over to a group of shady characters. The two lawmen noticed that the conversation centered on them. Anderson's conversation began with a whisper and ended with a shout: "They are cops." Patrons didn't pay much attention to this outburst as piano music, laughter and dancing muffled the outcry.[58]

A thug headwaiter named James "Slam Bang" DeLuccia came over and audaciously said, "Get out, get out." The enraged man didn't like McManus's questions and launched a roundhouse punch, striking McManus. However, the man was quickly brought under control, and Ullrich and McManus rose to their feet with pistols drawn. Standing on a chair, McManus shouted, "You're all under arrest." Eight prisoners were lined against the wall, and Ullrich took down their names and addresses. When everything settled down, Ullrich went into an adjoining room and phoned headquarters.[59]

While watching the prisoners, McManus turned his head momentarily, and Samual Alessi, the proprietor of the inn, bolted for the downstairs barroom. McManus took off after him, catching him at the foot of the stairs. "Sam had a gun in his right hand and pointed it at me," said McManus. "I grabbed the barrel with my left hand." A shot rang out, burning McManus's finger. While this was happening, the other prisoners fled, except for Alessi's brother, Anthony "Tony" D'Alessi, and James "Slam Bang" DeLuccia. They rushed down to the aid of Samual Alessi.[60]

Tony D'Alessi came from behind McManus and struck the trooper on the head. "As I was trying to get the gun," said McManus, "I was struck on the head with something hard." Another gunshot rang out. By now, Ullrich had rushed to the sound of the gunfire. Either D'Alessi or "Slam Bang" struck McManus over the head, releasing the hold McManus had. Then Alessi turned his attention toward Ullrich, firing a round into the trooper's face. The bullet struck Ullrich in the mouth, knocking him to the floor. Dazed and bleeding profusely, Ullrich rose up on his elbow and shot three rounds through his coat pocket, hitting Alessi in the chest. Alessi returned fire, striking Ullrich mortally in the head. Within minutes, state police personnel arrived at the inn and found Ullrich dead and McManus near death.[61]

Ullrich with dog, Sam Alessi in bed and Ruby Ullrich. *"Official Detective Stories" article by Isabel Stephen.*

Samual Alessi was brought by his crew to St. Joseph's Hospital in Paterson. It didn't take long for troopers to check the area hospitals and discover that a man was being treated in Paterson for gunshot wounds.[62]

McManus was brought to the All Souls' Hospital in Morristown, where he told investigators what had happened. With tears swelling up in his eyes, he told of Charley Ullrich rising up miraculously on an elbow and taking down the man who had tried to kill them. Ullrich's heroics saved McManus's life.[63]

With the names and addresses Ullrich had written down, coupled with McManus's statements, Alessi and DeLuccia were brought to justice. Five years later, Tony D'Alessi was found hiding out in Pennsylvania as an auto mechanic. However, after a haphazard trial, the prosecution couldn't prove its case, and Tony D'Alessi walked away a free man.[64]

At Trooper Charles E. Ullrich's funeral, thousands lined the streets in Paterson to pay their respects. Charles E. Ullrich was laid to rest in the Laurel Grove Cemetery in Totowa. He had no children.[65]

FORGOTTEN

Herman Gloor Jr. #240

May 3, 1899, was a cloudy day with rain falling periodically on the small borough of Haledon, New Jersey. It was a time when the horse and wagon could be seen coming down the street and mom stayed home while dad worked. William McKinley was president, and the citizens were looking forward to the new century. Haledon, a borough with fewer than three thousand people at the time, is positioned west of Paterson and east of Wayne and is only one square mile in size. On this dreary day, Herman Gloor Jr. was born. The Gloors were of Scottish descent, believed to have originated from the Dalriadan clans of Scotland. They resided at 371 Belmont Avenue.[66]

The community of Haledon was increasing, and there was a demand for modern equipment in the borough. On November 28, 1906, Haledon hosted a large parade to welcome its new fire department and firehouse. It was a large event, and it is believed that six-year-old Herman Gloor Jr. attended the parade. Gloor attended the public school in town, which he walked to every day.[67]

Another pivotal event for the borough of Haledon, one that the thirteen-year-old Gloor most certainly witnessed, was a large labor strike in 1912 at the Botto House. This site was the hub where thousands of people descended in protest.[68]

Little is known of Gloor's life until he was nineteen years old. It isn't until 1918 that we are provided with additional insight into his life. On February

Hermon Gloor Jr. #240.

23, 1918, Herman Gloor Jr. entered the United States Navy.[69] The World War was going on, and Gloor worked on the deck of a ship and learned navigation and vessel operation, eventually becoming a steersman. Progressing in his skills and knowledge, Gloor learned how to read navigational charts and maps and was promoted to quartermaster. In this capacity, he served as an assistant to commissioned officers. Other duties performed by him were deck operations and securing navigational supplies, charts and instruments. On October 12, 1920, at the age of twenty-one, Gloor was honorably discharged.[70]

After serving his country, Gloor became a chauffeur. However, he wasn't satisfied with this job and decided to apply for a position with the New Jersey State Police. Gloor wasn't alone, as many war veterans were making the transition from the military into law enforcement.[71] Gloor became a member of the eighth state police class, where he met a man with a similar background: Robert Coyle. Coyle, like Gloor, had served in the military and was a chauffeur.[72] Training was extremely difficult; however, there is no documentation of Gloor's performance. The depth of Gloor and Coyle's relationship isn't known either.[73]

On April 1, 1924, Gloor was given a badge and assigned to motorcycle patrol. He eventually was stationed out of the Tuckerton barracks. As a motorcycle trooper, he learned early that traffic enforcement can be as troubling as any other job performed by a trooper.[74]

On February 21 of either 1925 or 1926, Gloor stopped a woman named Theresa Jetter for speeding on White Horse Pike in the borough of Berlin. The trooper cautioned the woman and chose not to issue a summons. Jetter spread a rumor that she had avoided the fine by giving Gloor twenty-five dollars. Jetter was the wife of a well-known and respected inn owner in town, so word spread quickly.[75] An official state police probe was initiated and put the small community of Berlin in turmoil. Ultimately, Jetter was arrested and admitted to lying by signing an affidavit denying that the trooper had demanded any money. Gloor was exonerated, and Jetter was fined five dollars.[76]

On May 3, 1926, Herman Gloor Jr. turned twenty-seven. It was a day of celebration for him and his family. The time for grieving was just around the corner.[77]

On Sunday, May 9, history records that Herman Gloor was on patrol and responded to an emergency call on his Harley Davidson motorcycle. It was early in the morning, and while he was traveling on the Matawan and Freehold Road in Freehold, a motorist pulled out of a private driveway directly in the path of Gloor. Gloor died as a result.[78]

The service for Trooper Gloor took place on May 13, with throngs of people visiting the mortuary chapel. The crowd was so large that his body had to be moved to a larger location. Six touring cars were followed by an honor guard of fifty troopers. Gloor received full military honors. Harry Linderman, from the Coyle investigation, served as an honorary pallbearer. Also attending the service was thirty-two-year-old John Divers, who provided a motorcycle escort. Four years later, Divers would be the cause for another such gathering.[79]

Gloor was laid to rest in the Freehold cemetery and remained in an unmarked grave for sixty-seven years until it was brought to the attention of the Former Troopers Association, which paid for a headstone to be placed on the grave.[80]

VIEW OBSTRUCTION

Walter Arrowsmith #265

The name Arrowsmith is derived from a trade. An "arrowsmith" was a maker or seller of arrows. The name originates from Old English. In Lawrenceville, New Jersey, located in Mercer County, the Arrowsmiths were well known and resided in this community for years. The local cemetery bares this out.[81]

Walter Arrowsmith was born on August 7, 1902, in Lawrence Township in a part of town known as Port Mercer or Lawrenceville. The township of Lawrence dates back to 1697, when it was originally called Maidenhead. After the War of 1812, the township changed its name to honor one of the heroes of that war, James Lawrence.[82]

John and Anna Arrowsmith raised their children in this historic town known for its major thoroughfare, the Kings Highway. Now known as Route 202, the road played an important role during the Revolutionary War as George Washington used it to march to Princeton in January 1777. The Arrowsmiths had five children: Walter, George, Clark, William and Ethel. In 1915, they experienced a tragic loss with the death of six-year-old William. One can only imagine the pain and heartache John and Anna felt. Sadly, tragedy would besiege them again.[83]

Upon graduating from grammar school, Walter Arrowsmith became an automobile mechanic. Lawrence was an agricultural town that was slowly becoming a suburban community, and Arrowsmith thought it prudent to start his own business. He ventured into an industry that showed a lot of potential at the time.[84]

Walter Arrowsmith #265.

During the early twentieth century, ice manufacturing became a popular business. As a fact, ice manufacturing ranked ninth among American investors. Since Arrowsmith's side of town was near the Delaware and Raritan Canal, it provided an ample water supply.

Eventually, Arrowsmith realized that being an entrepreneur wasn't his calling.[85] Arrowsmith loved working on and riding automobiles and motorcycles, so with this passion in mind, he applied to the state police.[86] Walter Arrowsmith became a member of the tenth state police class and graduated on April 1, 1925. Trooper Walter Arrowsmith was given badge #265 and assigned a motorcycle. During his brief tenure with the organization, Arrowsmith was stationed in Sharptown. There, he became well known and liked by all. As a trooper, Arrowsmith performed exceptionally. When he was transferred to the Malaga Barracks, the young man was highly regarded by the citizens he served.[87]

Not much is documented of Arrowsmith's career. From April 1925 until August 1926, records document little but stress his dedication and professional conduct. The final entry in Arrowsmith's record is the event that led to his demise in the summer of 1926.[88]

The summer temperatures of 1926 were slightly above normal, and rainfall eluded most of the Northeast. It was a summer ideal for vacationing, and Arrowsmith made the most of it. Feeling fresh and rejuvenated from a month off, he was anxious to get back to patrol.[89]

After only a year as a motorcycle trooper, Arrowsmith relished his job. He enjoyed the freedom the open road had to offer: fresh country air blowing in his face, miles and miles of beautiful open fields that were filled with green pastures, large farmland and secluded wooded scenery. Motorcycle duty did, however, have a downside. Winter patrol could be brutal. There were primarily two modes of transportation within the state police during this period: the horse and motorcycle. Motorcycle troopers had to be extremely careful of ice and snow-covered roads. Furthermore, bearing the bitter winter temperatures could be excruciating while on a motorcycle. However, this was summer, and the weather was perfect. Arrowsmith was basking in it.[90]

On August 2, Arrowsmith was traveling through the rural township of Pilesgrove in Salem County. Pilesgrove was a farm community that housed fewer than two thousand residents. Running through the town was a stretch of road known as the Harding Highway. For various reasons, this road had several spots associated with a higher volume of auto accidents. One such spot was near the Hewitt farm.[91]

Unlike most of the farm homes in the area, Hewitt's sat close to the road. The Hewitt home obstructed a person's line of view from both the Harding Highway and the Richmantown Road. The house sat on an embankment higher than the road's elevation, which exacerbated the problem. The other three farms that met at this intersection were barely visible from the road.[92]

Arrowsmith was responding to an emergency call and was traveling east on the Harding Highway. The type of emergency is uncertain; newspaper accounts do not say, nor do state records indicate. Based on the history of the Harding Highway—with several accidents occurring on this day alone—it is believed that Arrowsmith was responding to an automobile accident.[93]

Arrowsmith knew that the intersection was troublesome, as did Charles A. Smiley. Smiley, a local resident, was fast approaching the intersection.[94] Traveling north on Richmantown Road, Smiley could see the Hewitt home and, to the left of it, the open view of the Harding Highway. As he approached, Smiley didn't see any traffic but blew his horn as a warning as he turned left onto the Harding Highway. Unfortunately, Arrowsmith was obstructed by the home, and Smiley pulled directly into the path of the trooper.[95]

Arrowsmith's motorcycle struck Smiley's car violently, catapulting him forcefully against the car. The trooper was brought to the Salem Hospital

Arrowsmith.

with head trauma and a broken jaw. For three days, the young man clung to life, with his brothers, George and Clark, and his dad at his side. On August 5, Arrowsmith passed away without ever having regained consciousness.[96]

Subsequently, Smiley was arrested and charged with manslaughter. The accident would later be determined by a jury to be "unavoidable."[97]

A day that should have been cause for celebration was now a day of grief and sadness. Walter Arrowsmith was laid to rest on what would have been his twenty-fourth birthday. The funeral was held in his hometown of Lawrenceville at the local Presbyterian church. He was buried in the Lawrenceville cemetery. Walter Arrowsmith was unmarried and had no children.[98]

"OLD MALADY"

David Z. Ernst #305

David Z. Ernst was born on Wednesday, February 7, 1900, in a small town just north of the Mason-Dixon line. Waynesboro, Pennsylvania, was a community with only 5,300 residents at the time of Ernst's birth. Settled in 1949, the town is named after the great Revolutionary War general Anthony Wayne. This rural industrial community primarily consisted of residents who worked building engines, boilers and related materials or were wood- and ironworkers. Waynesboro was a quiet setting of middle-class citizens, to which the Ernst family belonged.[99]

Ernst is a German surname dating back to Bavaria, where the family of Ernst is believed to have originated. The name Ernst means "serious person." During the mid-seventeenth century, German settlers began to arrive in what is now the United States. One of the earliest settlers of the Ernst name was Felix Ernst, who is known to have moved to Pennsylvania in 1744. David Ernst's personal family history isn't known. It is almost certain that he was a descendant of Felix Ernst. Nothing further is known of his upbringing or educational background.[100]

At the age of nineteen, David Ernst began his career in law enforcement as a police officer for the Lehigh Valley Railroad Police. In 1846, the Lehigh Valley Railroad was constructed for the speedy transportation of anthracite coal. The railroad was often called the "Route of the Black Diamond," referring to the coal it transported. The railroad line ran from New York Harbor to Buffalo, New York, and passed through the Allentown-

David Z. Ernst #305.

Bethlehem-Easton metropolitan area, commonly called the Lehigh Valley. As a policeman for the railroad, Ernst was responsible for apprehending trespassers and investigating crimes. Ernst worked six years for the railroad and, during his tenure, served with distinction.[101]

In the summer of 1926, Ernst graduated from the thirteenth state police class. By this time, the state police had grown to be a few hundred troopers strong. Ernst was assigned to the Berlin Sub-Station and would serve at several stations throughout his career. At five feet, eleven inches and weighing nearly 180 pounds, Ernst was physically imposing, and his work ethic and natural abilities made it easy for him to assimilate into the "outfit."[102]

Ernst moved to South Plainfield, New Jersey, which is the site of the first transatlantic mail flight and consisted mostly of farmers and day laborers.[103]

The year was now 1927, and the twenty-six-year-old appeared to be in excellent health, with a bright future. Or so his medical examination revealed. Nothing was noted other than a very distinct "birthmark on the front of his body." It was a visible mark of a past trauma. But he also had an imperceptible injury that went undiscovered.[104]

On August 2, 1927, David Ernst was riding his state police Harley Davidson when he suffered a seizure and crashed into a sand pile. Fortunately, he wasn't going fast, and the incident was more embarrassing than serious. Neither Ernst nor anyone else knew what had caused the sudden attack. Everyone was alarmed by the mysterious episode, and officials placed him on light administrative duty.[105]

The following day, Ernst was signing troopers in and out of the station and answering the phone. He seemed fine and was in good spirits. At 10:30 a.m., while on the phone, Ernst fell to the floor and never regained consciousness.[106] Trooper Ernst was brought to the Cooper Hospital in Camden, New Jersey, where drastic attempts to save his life were futile. David Ernst died at 1:10 a.m. on August 4.[107]

The autopsy was conducted by Dr. Ewing and the "County Physician," with the cause of death listed as "Uremic Convulsions, coupled with an old fracture of the skull." State police officials tried to have a more detailed clarification of the "old fracture," but in a memo dated June 21—presumably the next summer—the cause of death was still extremely vague, saying that the death was from an "old malady." A newspaper article stated that Ernst had died from an attack of convulsions caused by a fracture of the skull suffered when he was two years old.[108]

Trooper David Z. Ernst's funeral was held on Sunday, August 7, and he was interred at the Green Hill Cemetery in Waynesboro, Pennsylvania.[109]

ADOPTED

Joseph A. Smith #231

Little is contained in the state police museum files on Joseph A. Smith. It is said that he was born in Passaic, New Jersey, on August 31, 1897. The surname Smith comes from either Dutch, English, German, Irish or Scottish descent, making it impossible to determine what ethnicity he was. Shortly after his birth, for reasons not known, Smith was adopted by the Jones family of New Britain, Connecticut. Smith's adoptive parents' first names are also not known. His adoptive sister's name was Eva, and she was his sole beneficiary.[110]

Joseph Smith grew up in New Britain, which at the time was known for its hardware manufacturing. He remained there until 1907, when the Joneses moved to New Jersey. They briefly lived in Passaic before settling in Jersey City.[111]

Presumably, the Jones family was Catholic, as they sent Joseph to St. Bridget's Parochial School in Jersey City. After graduating, Smith worked as a clerk (type isn't known). In December 1916, in the middle of the First World War, Joseph Smith enlisted in the United States military. He served in the army from December 17, 1916, until June 13, 1923. His record of conduct and military experiences aren't known. Records do indicate that Smith rose to the rank of second lieutenant and was honorably discharged in 1923.[112]

After his military service, Smith applied to the state police. It was a natural transition requiring the same physical standards. The state police had been in existence for a little over a year when Smith entered training. At the academy, Smith met Charles E. Ullrich, and they became bunkmates. As

Joseph A. Smith #231.

the weeks passed, Smith and Ullrich struggled through the intense training at the West Trenton facility. Their hard work and perseverance paid off, and they graduated on September 1, 1923.[113]

On August 5, 1927, Smith was working for the governor's day celebration out of the Farmingdale Station. On this particular day, he was directing traffic by the railroad tracks outside the Sea Girt military base. It was a strenuous day, as over thirty thousand people gathered to celebrate. Smith worked all day without any relief. Throngs of people were ushered out and observed the slender trooper moving traffic along. Afterward, Smith hopped on his state police Harley Davidson and drove to his home in Point Pleasant, a small beach community with beautiful sand beaches for relaxing after such a long day. Moreover, the nightlife was perfect for a bachelor.[114]

Smith invited fellow troopers Cyril Dalton #304 and Earl Smith #92 to eat at his home, and they sat and enjoyed each other's company over dinner. The three separated and resumed their duties, with Joseph entering State Highway 35 and heading north. At the foot of the Manasquan River Bridge, Joseph Smith struck the rear of a large truck. Incidentally, the driver, William J. Hicks, was a friend of the trooper. It was said the impact was so intense that the force crushed Smith's chest. Smith died five minutes after arriving at the hospital.[115]

Trooper Smith's body was transported to New Britain, Connecticut, where the funeral service was held. Joseph A. Smith was buried in Fairview Cemetery in that city. He was thirty years old.[116]

COLD-BLOODED MURDER

Peter W. Gladys #378

He sleeps in peace by the side of his comrades who have given their all to the cause. Time may assuage the grief in the hearts of those who mourn for him. But his memory will carry its influence to the men in the service and remind them of their responsibility of supporting the principles for which this young life was given. [117]

Stephen and Mary (née Swistack) Gladys were born in Russia and immigrated to the United States. There they settled in Stanhope, New Jersey, which is nestled in rural Sussex County. Stanhope was part of the larger Byram Township and was a hotbed for iron manufacturing and related businesses. The iron industry supported the locals with ample employment. It was a quaint community with a general store, blacksmith shop, sawmills and gristmills. Another feature in town was the Morris Canal, built by the Morris Canal and Banking Company as a large waterway running through New Jersey. The canal was completed in 1831 and provided a speedy means to transport food and goods. On March 21, 1906, Peter Gladys was born into this environment. Peter was the second child; his older brother John had been born in 1903. [118]

Stephen Gladys supported his family working at the Atlas Powder Company. Atlas manufactured explosives needed for extracting iron ore. It was a secure but dangerous job that put the food on the table. Unfortunately, a terrible explosion in 1908 killed Stephen Gladys and left a devastating

Peter W. Gladys #378.

effect on the family. Growing up without a father was tough for John and Peter Gladys. Mary raised them as best she could.[119]

Peter and John attended the local school, and Peter proved to be athletically inclined. He enjoyed sports, especially basketball. After grammar school, he attended the regional high school in Netcong. During his school days, Gladys was considered by many to be a "great athlete." The state police was making a name for itself during Gladys's high school tenure, as it was formed during his sophomore year. By his senior year, the state police was being called an elite outfit. Whether this was a catalyst for him to join the organization is not known. After high school, Gladys began working odd jobs from 1926 until 1928. Peter was a quiet person and a wonderful role model who enjoyed playing with the younger kids in the neighborhood.[120]

In early 1928, Gladys applied to the New Jersey State Police. Training began on June 16, and it is here that he met another accomplished athlete, John Madden of Pennsylvania. Together, they endured the grueling training of horse riding, sit-ups, push-ups and running, coupled with difficult classroom instruction. On September 15, 1928, members of the seventeenth class graduated, with Gladys being assigned to the Barnbertville Barracks. Madden was transferred to south Jersey.[121] After Barnbertville, Gladys moved to the Hightstown Barracks. Hightstown borough is the central-most point in New Jersey, located in Mercer County.[122]

Three days after Christmas, history records show that Gladys was back on patrol. It was a cold, active Friday night, and a local troublemaker named David Ware was acting up. Ware was a "burly" man with anger problems. This night, the Bahamian-born migrant worker assaulted his girlfriend, Pansy Keaton, as he had done many times before. A call went out to the New Jersey State Police about the domestic disturbance.[123]

The couple lived in Allentown, a Monmouth County community with only seven hundred residents. Domestic disputes are often difficult because they are fueled by passion and, at times, uncontrollable rage. While responding to such calls, a trooper must act as a psychologist, sociologist and a cop all rolled into one. Understanding relationships, human behavior and patterns of social interaction requires a higher degree of maturity and experience than a six-month tenured trooper can offer. Experience is the key to becoming a knowledgeable worker; the more experience one has, the better suited one is to handle the next similar situation. Time is one key ingredient of experience. This was a compound that Gladys did not have.[124]

Gladys responded to the call and arrested Ware. The trooper then decided to transport the man to the local magistrate for immediate arraignment, which was standard procedure for the time. If Ware was searched by the trooper, it was a lackluster search. To make matters worse, Ware was placed in the front seat un-cuffed, with his girlfriend in the back seat. Ware was fully cooperative and gave no indication of trouble.[125]

Traveling on the isolated Robbinsville-Windsor Road, Ware and Keaton began to argue. Tolerant to some point, Gladys eventually tried to put an end to the disturbance and pulled off to the side of the road. The out-of-control, six-foot, two-hundred-pound man was too much for Gladys, as Ware pulled out a straight-edged shaving razor and sliced the trooper's throat. Dropping the weapon that spilled the lifeblood of Gladys, the crazed Ware took the trooper's gun and shot him. Then he grabbed the ammo belt and fled, escaping into an open field while Keaton, scared and bewildered, found refuge at a friend's house.[126]

Within hours, dozens of troopers and civilian volunteers were searching the area. The United States Navy provided assistance with a J-3 airship. Residents were outraged, and there became a threat of civil unrest as citizens were stating that they were going to lynch the "Negro."[127]

Ware avoided authorities by hiding in a swamp near the Camden and Amboy railroad tracks and hopped a freight train into Carteret, New Jersey.

Picture from the New Jersey State Police
Triangle.

While walking the streets trying to find a place to hide, Ware spotted two Carteret police officers. Hiding in plain sight, with a bloodstained shirt, he asked the inept cops for directions to the nearest boardinghouse. They were helpful and provided the necessary details.[128]

Ware checked himself into a boardinghouse and was befriended by a man named Alexander Middleton. Middleton provided the hungry man with food. Ware, believing that Middleton was a newfound friend, told him that he had murdered a Jersey trooper. He gave Middleton the gun and offered to sell it to him for four dollars. Middleton took the weapon, promising to pay the fee later.[129]

The murderous deed didn't sit well with Middleton, and two days later, he reported it to Lieutenant Ray J. Dowling of the Carteret Police Department. Dowling went to the boardinghouse and, with pistol in hand, burst into Ware's upstairs room. Ware was crazed no more and surrendered without incident. Inside the room was Gladys's revolver and remnants of a "bloodstained" shirt that had been set on fire in an attempt to destroy the evidence.[130]

The funeral for the twenty-two-year-old took place on New Year's Eve 1928. The service was held at St. Michael's Church in Stanhope. Peter Gladys was buried in the Union Cemetery in town. Gladys was unmarried and had no children.[131]

In February 1929, David Ware was found guilty, and he went to the electric chair on May 5, 1929.[132]

UNDOCUMENTED

John Madden #383

Shenandoah is located in the lower part of Schuylkill County, Pennsylvania, and is part of the coal region. Settled between 1820 and 1835, records indicate that one of the earliest settlers to Shenandoah was Peter Kehley, who discovered anthracite coal in a nearby stream. During the Civil War, anthracite coal mines began to sprout up, and as a result, Shenandoah began to develop.[133]

Initially, an influx of English, Welsh, Irish and German immigrants flocked to the area. At the turn of the twentieth century, people from the eastern and southern European countries moved into the region. By the early 1900s, the once wooded area had become a metropolis with nearly thirty thousand people.[134]

Census records indicate that the Madden family was residing in Shenandoah as early as the late 1800s. John Madden, of the seventeenth state police class, was born in Shenandoah on October 9, 1905. His father, in all likelihood, was a miner. An 1890 census record shows that the Maddens were living at 20 Bower Street. James, twenty-six; Thomas, twenty-eight; and Dominick, eighteen, presumably all brothers, were the only Maddens present in the community. James and Thomas were miners, while Dominick was a laborer. It is unclear which Madden was John's father. State police records indicate that Minnie Madden was John's mother.[135]

John's father was of Irish descent, as the names Madden and O'Madden are derivatives of the Gaelic O Madaidhin. The family of O'Madden is from

John Madden #383.

the banks of the Shannon River, where they exist to this day. The Maddens of Pennsylvania didn't have much money. John's father is presumed to have died at any early age, as John was sent to the Girard College in Philadelphia, Pennsylvania, a boarding school for students grades one through twelve for families with a single parent and limited financial resources. While in school, John Madden loved sports and was known as "an accomplished athlete."[136]

In 1921, when John was sixteen, Minnie Madden moved her family to Elizabeth, New Jersey. Presumably, Minnie sought more prosperous employment, as the city had more to offer for a woman than the mining borough of Shenandoah.[137]

After graduating grammar school, Madden learned the trade of carpentry. Madden worked as a carpenter until applying for the state police. On May 14, 1926, Madden received word that he had been accepted into the State Police Academy. He, along with Peter Gladys, began training on June 16 and continued throughout the summer until their graduation on September 15. The two parted ways; Gladys went north and Madden went south.[138]

After his probation period, Madden was transferred to the Deerfield Barracks. Deerfield Township is located in Cumberland County and is part of southern New Jersey. Deerfield was one of the initial townships incorporated in New Jersey on February 21, 1798, and boasted only 1,500 residents.[139]

Like Gladys, Madden was struck down in the prime of his life. State police archives tell little of John Madden. What this young man did has been lost with the passing of time.[140]

Throughout his brief career, John Madden worked as a motorcycle trooper, an assignment that proved time and again to be a deadly one. Riding the open road was enjoyable, as Walter Arrowsmith knew, but the safety helmet of the '20s was not what it is today. Furthermore, motorists were just learning to drive, and inattentive motorists caused the demise of many troopers. While in the academy, Madden was cautioned on the hazards of the open road, highlighted by names such as Marshall, Gloor, Arrowsmith and Smith. As such, state police recruits went through rigorous motorcycle training.[141]

In March 1929, the state police was wrapping up its first decade. It had been a difficult period for the newly formed organization; three troopers were murdered, and five lost their lives while on motorcycle patrol. Schwarzkopf, along with his staff, had hoped the decade would close without another loss of life. This was not to be.[142]

March 1, 1929, was a cold day with nothing out of the ordinary other than the fact that in the national news, Charles Lindbergh and his fiancée, Anne Morrow, had to make an emergency landing in Mexico City. In New Jersey, Judge Albert H. Holland of Morristown was lecturing at state police headquarters in Wilberta on duties relating to the courts, securing evidence and other police matters. Meanwhile, in south Jersey, Trooper John Madden was riding his Harley through the rural community of Deerfield. While on patrol, he was met with an accident that claimed his life. Dr. Lyon determined the cause of death to be a fractured skull. Madden passed away in the Bridgeton Hospital at 5:30 p.m. on March 3, 1929.[143]

John Madden's sole beneficiary was his mother, Minnie. John Madden was buried in the city of Elizabeth at the Evergreen Cemetery.[144]

INFECTION

John D. Divers #127

John Divers was born on July 22, 1894, in the rural community of Blairstown, New Jersey, which is nestled in the hills of Warren County. Originally called Gravel Hill, in 1839 the town's name was changed to honor entrepreneur and railroad magnate John Insley Blair. Nothing is known of John Divers's parents other than that they were from the area of Blairstown. Divers grew up here and, as an adult, chose to call the nearby town of Columbia his home.[145]

Columbia is an unincorporated portion of Knowlton Township that comprises the eastern region of the Lehigh Valley. The township of Knowlton is part of Warren County and dates back to 1798. Knowlton is a beautiful community with open farmland and panoramic views of the Delaware River. At one time, five railroads crisscrossed through the town, with one of them, Lehigh Valley, bringing David Ernst #305 into town as he rode the line as a railroad cop.[146]

As a child, Divers attended the local school and graduated from Blairstown High School. Afterward, Divers enrolled at the McCan Junior College but left less than two years later.[147]

By 1914, Divers had begun working in the Columbia area, first as an electrician and then as an automobile mechanic. The young man worked until a pivotal moment in American history occurred in late 1917: the First World War. President Woodrow Wilson, elected because he advocated peace, had no choice but to enter the United States in the conflict because of

John D. Divers #127.

Germany's unrelenting submarine warfare. Our formal entry came in April 1917. Seven months later, on Wednesday, November 21, Divers entered the army. Whether he enlisted or was drafted isn't certain. Divers served with the 308th Field Artillery in Battery F. The World War ended in 1918, and Divers completed his service on May 21, 1919.[148]

From May 1919 until his entry into the state police, little is known of John Divers. It is believed that after the army, Divers attended a trade school in New York.[149]

John Divers certainly read of the newly formed state police and the successful graduation of the first troopers in December 1921. Presumably impressed by the accolades the state police was getting, Divers applied to the department. H. Normal Schwarzkopf had done an outstanding job creating the organization, and now he was trying to iron out the wrinkles. Police work isn't easy; Schwarzkopf needed to turn his troopers into lawmen. It would take time, and it would come with a price.[150]

While in the academy, John Divers was instructed on forestry, police practice, first aid and fish and game violations. To this day, many citizens of New Jersey don't have a full understanding of the authority that state troopers have. Troopers are given a great deal of power, above and beyond the local law official. The fact that troopers are also game wardens is one illustration of this authority. John Divers became a trooper on Saturday, April 1, 1922.[151] Another trooper graduating this day was Matthew McManus #144, who would have a short and troubling career.[152]

Some troopers began on horseback; for Divers, it was a motorcycle. The first insight into his career comes in May 1926, when history records him escorting the hearse that carried Herman Gloor's body. After motorcycle patrol, Divers moved to a horse, and he eventually became a saddler and was promoted to corporal saddler. In April 1928, a law was passed reorganizing the "outfit," and positions such as signal sergeant, medical sergeant, stable sergeant, corporal clerk, signal corporal, corporal saddler and corporal horse-shoer were abolished. Apparently, the state police did away with specific position titles but not the responsibilities. The law simply put a more generalized rank structure into place. With this transition, many were able to keep their ranks, and Divers was one of them.[153]

Divers was a capable trooper and moved through the ranks quickly. Toward the end of his career, he was given command of a barracks. Records state that in December 1929, Corporal John Divers was the station commander of the Newton Station. Station commanders are the equivalent of a modern-day police chief, as they run the station operation. Newton Station was responsible for policing the southern portion of Sussex County. Most communities in Sussex County did not have local police, and the Jersey trooper was the only law. In fact, this holds true to the present day. The Jersey trooper can still be seen throughout Sussex County. This location was perfect for Divers, as his Columbia residence was nearby. Then, on Christmas Eve 1929, Divers was given a tentative promotion to sergeant and transferred to central New Jersey (Troop C).[154]

On Wednesday, January 1, 1930, the thirty-five-year-old received his promotion and took command of the Columbus Barracks in Burlington County. Columbus was originally called Encroaching Corners; however, in the 1700s, the name was changed to Black Horse after a popular tavern. The name remained through the American Revolution, but when the tavern was renamed Columbus, the town's name followed the pub. Even though he was a station commander, Divers stayed actively engaged in the police function, and his diligence and devotion to this cause is highlighted by the events of January 19, 1930.[155]

It was a cold Sunday night in January when Captain Frank Gilbert, a ranking officer for the nearby Burlington Police Department, called Divers. Gilbert needed help in hunting down a wanted criminal. Divers assigned Trooper Lyle Reynolds #444 and went along to assist.[156]

At the Burlington Police Headquarters, Captain Gilbert and Patrolman Hance said that the subject of their investigation was a man named William Ware, a local troublemaker with warrants for burglary, theft and larceny. Together, the investigation led the lawmen to the home of Ware's father in Burlington.[157]

Upon arriving at the East Federal Street home, they were greeted by William Ware's father, James, who was drunk. With Prohibition in effect, this was a problem. After a brief conversation, it was determined that William was hiding inside. Entering the house, William was found and placed under arrest. While the lawmen were searching the home, James became enraged and abusive. He was placed under arrest, but not without a struggle. By the time it ended, Ware had received numerous lacerations. In struggling with Ware, a scab from a minor cut was ripped off Diver's finger, and Ware's blood entered the wound.[158]

Arriving at the Burlington Police Headquarters, everyone washed up, as it was a well-known fact that James Ware had syphilis. After washing his hands, Divers chose not to seek medical attention.[159] Local officials knew that Ware was extremely contagious and notified the New Jersey Department of Health Bureau of Venereal Disease Control in Trenton, New Jersey.[160]

A week later, Divers's finger began showing signs of infection, and on Friday, February 21, 1930, Divers's tests revealed that he had contracted

Divers is standing on right.

syphilis. Once notified, the state police fumigated the Columbus Barracks and placed Divers on sick leave. An inquiry into the facts and circumstances surrounding the illness was immediately begun.[161]

On Wednesday, March 12, 1930, Pathologist Dr. Henry B. Decker authored a letter stating that he had examined John Divers and believed that Divers had contracted the disease from Ware. "His history," Decker wrote, "was that in making an arrest, some weeks previously, he had injured his finger on the skin of the person arrested. This is a perfectly logical explanation of the infection." Decker concluded his letter: "It is [my] opinion…that this infection was acquired in the line of duty."[162]

By April 1930, John Divers's condition had become serious, and he was admitted to the Easton Hospital in Pennsylvania. Medical expenses began to mount, and the hospital inquired about payment. On Tuesday, April 22, Colonel H. Norman Schwarzkopf replied: "We are advised by Dr. Haggerty that you request confirmation in writing concerning responsibility for bills of Sergeant Divers…The Department will assume any expense incurred in connection with the Sergeant's case."[163]

On Friday, May 2, 1931, John Divers died in his hospital bed at the age of thirty-five. He was married with no children.[164]

CAUTION

Peter William Ignatz #530

Send Trooper to home of Tpr. Ignatz…and advise parents that their son, Peter William Ignatz has been killed.
—teletype message, March 4, 1931[165]

Peter Ignatz was born on October 17, 1908, in Perth Amboy, New Jersey, to John and Sophia. "The City by the Bay" was growing as droves of people flocked to the beaches and immigrants moved here because of the factory work available from such companies as A. Hall and Sons Terra Cotta and Copper Works Smelting.[166]

John and Sophia Ignatz had three children: Helen, Mary and Peter. John had a child from a prior marriage, also named John. John Ignatz's vocation isn't known, but it is likely that he, too, was a factory worker.[167]

Peter Ignatz graduated grammar school but left high school after freshman year. At fifteen, he entered the working world, which at the time was not an uncommon practice.[168] Ignatz was hired by the Sarnoff-Irving Hat Store, which was a franchise spread throughout several states that sold fine hats and shoes. The young man worked here for a number of years and enjoyed the job, but the stock market crash in October 1929 changed his destiny.[169]

Ignatz applied to and was accepted into the state police academy. On July 1, 1930, Ignatz graduated from the twenty-second class. His first assignment was the Flemington Barracks in Troop B.[170]

Peter William Ignatz #530.

On a cold day in December 1930, Peter Ignatz discovered the danger of motorcycle patrol personally. While on patrol on Stanton Station Road, a vehicle turned directly in front of him. Ignatz walked away with a laceration on his head and three stitches. The trooper's "leather helmet" was credited with saving his life and lessening the severity of the accident.[171]

Three months had passed since that December day, and Ignatz's stitches had been removed and replaced by a scare—a reminder of the danger he faced. It was March 1931, and Ignatz was working out of the Morristown Headquarters. March 4 was a miserable, cold, dark and dreary day with a combination of snow and rain falling on the countryside. Roadways were dangerously wet and snow covered, which made driving conditions horrible.[172]

As Ignatz was heading out of Morristown Headquarters to investigate an accident, station troopers cautioned about taking a bike and offered a car instead. Ignatz refused and rode out on his Harley Davidson. Presumably, remarks were made about his decision because a person overheard Ignatz say, "I might come back with only one arm." Whether a premonition or a joke, it cast an eerie spell over the dark and dreary day.[173]

Sometime between 1:30 and 1:45 p.m., Ignatz arrived at the accident on Mendham Road. He spoke with the two drivers, Clifford Mills and Van

Goder, and viewed the damage to their vehicles. Both had minor damage. Ignatz wrote the report, and the drivers were sent on their way.[174]

About 2:40 p.m., Ignatz started back to headquarters and was riding east on the wooded Mendham Road in the township of Morris when he spotted a speeder. Ignatz twisted his throttle and raced to catch the lawbreaker. As he moved closer to the violator, he came upon a bend in the road where a truck was rounding the curve. Apparently, the truck came partially into the trooper's lane, causing his motorcycle to strike the truck. Death was instant for the young lawman. The leather helmet that had saved his life back in December was no match for the cold hard metal of the truck.[175]

The funeral for Peter William Ignatz was held on Sunday, March 8, with a small service at his parents' home on Florida Grove Road in Keasby. The formal service took place at St. Michael's Church on the corner of Amboy and Hall Avenues in Perth Amboy.[176] Peter William Ignatz was laid to rest in St. Michael's Cemetery in Perth Amboy. He was twenty-two years old.[177]

ALLEGATIONS

Leonard P. McCandless #561

Leonard Paul McCandless Jr. was born in Cedarville, New Jersey, on July 24, 1908, to Leonard Sr. and Mary Jane McCandless. Cedarville dates back to 1748, when a portion of Salem County was sectioned off to make Cumberland. The name McCandless is either of Irish or Scottish descent. They were likely of Irish descent based on the derivative spelling of their name. Of the six McCandless children, Leonard and his brother George are the only two identified. His four sisters' names aren't known. Leonard Sr. was an avid horseman who used to clean the streets on horseback. The McCandlesses resided in Bridgeton in Cumberland County, and Leonard went through the school system there, graduating from Bridgeton High School.[178]

In 1926, the eighteen-year-old McCandless was a chauffeur for a packaging company in Millville, New Jersey. The company was owned by John M. Bailey and operated in the city of Millville. McCandless worked here until his acceptance into the state police.[179]

When McCandless entered training in the summer of 1930, the state police had grown considerably in size. The force had risen above two hundred troopers and was now providing fingerprint services, crime labs and civil identification and, for the first time, had a detective bureau. Members of the twenty-third class were welcomed into the department on Wednesday, October 1, 1930. McCandless was assigned to Troop C.[180]

Leonard Paul McCandless #561.

McCandless was bright and likable and learned his job quickly. He was a good-looking man who was strong, polite and a man of integrity and character. A local engineer wrote to the superintendent telling of McCandless's professionalism and deportment, saying that few police agencies had an officer like McCandless.[181] The trooper was a natural on a Harley Davidson, and it didn't take long before he became a skilled motorcyclist. McCandless was sent to the Toms River Station and continued with his motorcycle duties.[182]

By the summer of 1931, McCandless's father was disabled, making it impossible for him to work. The junior Leonard became the breadwinner and supported his family. It was a little over a year after the stock market crash, and times were tough. To McCandless, his family was everything. He lived with them at a quaint home at 423 South Avenue in Bridgeton.[183]

On June 28, 1931, history finds Trooper McCandless enjoying a nice Sunday afternoon patrolling through the seaside community of Berkeley Township. Part of McCandless's appeal was his ability to connect with those he served. As such, McCandless made several stops throughout his shift. His first was to see his girlfriend, a young beauty who worked in Berkeley at a place called Sleights. All that is known of this woman is her last name, which was Eckhart. The two lovebirds talked for a while in the parking lot, and then McCandless rode off.[184]

During the remainder of the day, McCandless made a few stops, first at the Toms River Station and then at a local garage. Abe Novin was a state police mechanic who said that McCandless was the best bike driver he had seen. McCandless spoke with Novin for a while and then resumed patrol. The next entry in McCandless's patrol is marked shortly after 4:00 p.m.[185]

While heading south on Route 4 in Berkeley, McCandless spotted a speeding vehicle. The violator was a few hundred feet ahead of him, so the trooper twisted the throttle and sped off in pursuit. The sound of the roaring Harley was heard by patrons and workers as it approached Sleights, the place he had earlier visited. All eyes were directed toward the road as this impressive figure in uniform flew by, chasing the motorist. When McCandless passed a slow-moving vehicle, he didn't see an oncoming car traveling north, and he was struck head-on. The crash was quick and deadly.[186]

Trooper Leonard Paul McCandless Jr. was buried on July 2, 1931, with a service being held at his parents' home and at the First Methodist Episcopal Church in Cedarville. He was laid to rest in the Cedar Hill Cemetery in Cedarville, New Jersey. He was twenty-two years old.[187]

Seven years later, George McCandless #666 followed in his brother's footsteps and graduated from the twenty-seventh class along with John Gregerson, Frank Trainor and Walter Otte.[188]

HIT AND RUN

Michael J. Beylon #318

The city of Philadelphia is one of the most treasured places in the United States, for it is there that our nation was born. Important American figures such as Thomas Jefferson, Benjamin Franklin and George Washington walked the hallowed streets here. Several notable figures from the annals of the state police came from this great city as well. In 1898, Robert Coyle #238 was born here, and five years later, on March 6, 1903, so was Michael J. Beylon. Beylon's parents, Michael and Mary, had eight children: Michael, Joseph, John, Julie, Mary (died as an infant), Ann, Elizabeth and Mary. They were of Czechoslovakian descent. The Beylons moved to Elizabeth, New Jersey, sometime during Michael's grammar school years.[189]

The Beylons had a modest four-bedroom house at 412 South Broad Street in Elizabeth, New Jersey. They converted the upstairs attic into bedrooms to accommodate their large family. The couple also took in their niece and nephew, Elizabeth and John Rescoe. Michael learned early in life the importance of a close family; with eight children living under one roof, there was no other alternative. Michael Beylon Sr. was a rigger by trade and worked in the port of Elizabeth for the Standard Oil Company. The Beylons were of Catholic faith, and all their children went to St. Mary's School in the city. In 1917, at the age of fourteen, Michael Beylon completed his grammar school education and began working.[190]

By 1923, the twenty-year-old was working with his father as a rigger. It was a physically demanding job that was hot in the summer and cold in the winter.

Michael Beylon #318.

Beylon developed a newfound respect for his father's vocation. At this time, Beylon enlisted in the New Jersey National Guard. During his tenure, he served as part of Company B for the 114th Infantry. The military bearing and leadership learned proved an asset for him and made him a credible candidate for the New Jersey State Police. At the age of twenty-three, Beylon left the guard.[191]

By now, Mike Beylon had grown to be a good-looking man with a masculine build, standing at six feet, four inches. Beylon's sister Betty says, "The ladies loved him." While growing up, "Mickey" (as his sisters called him) remained close with his siblings. Betty says that he was especially fond of his parents.[192]

By 1926, the state police had been policing the rural communities for five years with Colonel Schwarzkopf still at the helm. More and more, on horse or motorcycle, those impressive figures wearing military-style uniforms were seen riding through town, securing law and order. No longer were citizens satisfied with the local constabulary. If they had their druthers, a trooper would be in every town.[193]

Members of the fourteenth class had to endure their training in the blistering winter cold and qualified with their pistols on what is now the site of the New Jersey State Police Museum in West Trenton.[194]

On March 16, 1927, "Big Mike," as his academy classmates called him, was given badge #318 and assigned to the southern portion of New Jersey.[195]

"Big Mike" (left) comparing uniforms.

After becoming a trooper, Beylon met an attractive woman named Romaine Virgina Bowman. The two dated, fell in love and, in the winter of 1929, Romaine became pregnant. Not yet wed, the two started to plan their wedding. However, a turn of events in early 1930 changed everything.[196]

Big Mike Beylon had a temper, and it got the best of him on March 25, 1930, when he struck a prisoner in the Toms River prosecutor's office. Officials were appalled, and the state police filed criminal charges against the twenty-seven-year-old trooper.[197]

Throughout the summer of 1930, while preparing for the birth of their child, Beylon's fate was uncertain. Happiness came on August 19 with the birth of their son, Robert Beylon. However, troubles mounted when formal state police administrative charges were filed.[198] Eventually, the charges were dismissed, but on January 15, 1931, a civil jury awarded the prisoner $250—a hefty sum equaling approximately 14 percent of Beylon's salary. Then, on June 19, 1931, Beylon was suspended without pay for nine months.[199]

By 1932, Beylon was back working at the Somerville Station in Bridgewater. This two-story stone structure that sits on what is known today as State Highway 22 is rich in state police history, and some seventy years later, it is still a working station.[200]

Monday, February 22, 1932, is a day forever etched in state police history. Trooper Beylon and Trooper Alton W. Geran #400 were out on motorcycle patrol and stopped a speeder in the town of North Plainfield. Trooper Geran began issuing a warning to the driver, while Big Mike told Geran that he would see him in a bit and mounted his bike.[201]

Beylon rolled down Highway 29 (now Route 22) on his bike. The moonlight cast his silhouette on the ground as he thundered down the road. Traffic was moving along nicely when, all of a sudden, it came to a complete stop. Beylon didn't react quickly enough and ran into the back of a Dodge Roadster. He fell onto the lane of travel, where an oncoming vehicle ran him over. The driver of that car never stopped.[202] The investigation never led to an apprehension of the hit-and-run motorist. Some believe that the Lindbergh kidnapping, a week later, caused a shift of resources to the more publicity-driven case.[203]

The funeral for Michael J. Beylon took place on February 25, 1931, at his home on South Broad Street in Elizabeth. A Mass followed at St. Joseph's Roman Catholic Church on Division Street in that city. Michael J. Beylon was twenty-eight years old.[204]

A happy postscript to the Beylon story is that his son, Robert, went on to become a detective with the Union County prosecutor's office. His grandson, Robert, is also in law enforcement.[205]

TROOPER AND THE MYSTERY WOMAN

John Ressler #494

John Ressler was born on Tuesday, January 8, 1907, in New York City. On the day of his birth, Teddy Roosevelt was president of the United States and George McClellan Jr. was the mayor of the city. It was common to see a horse and wagon riding down the street, and the towering skyscrapers New York is now known for had not yet been built. Nonetheless, New York was a bustling city with manufacturing, commerce and boatloads of immigrants arriving at Ellis Island. The Ressler family was of German descent and lived in the city until John was two. The Resslers had ten children, five boys and five girls.[206]

In 1909, the Resslers moved to Newark, New Jersey. In the late nineteenth century, German migrants had flocked to the city, and many set up newspaper businesses. There is a strong possibility that Ressler's father worked in this profession. In 1919, the Resslers moved to 221 Liberty Avenue in Hillside, New Jersey.[207]

At fourteen years old, John Ressler entered the working world, first as a milkman delivering on horseback and then as a driver and a pipe fitter. In 1927, at the age of twenty, he became a chauffeur. He worked doing this until 1929, when he entered the state police academy.[208]

In mid-1929, members of the twenty-first class began training. Ressler was a small man who stood at five feet, eight inches, weighed 160 pounds and had blue eyes and a ruddy complexion. He was one of the smallest in his class. On October 1, 1929, three weeks before the stock market crashed, Ressler's class graduated. As many Americans began feeling the effects of

John J. Ressler #494.

the stock market crash, Ressler was relishing in his new job. He was assigned motorcycle patrol.[209]

By December 1930, Ressler was working in the Mays Landing, Atlantic County area. On December 16, Trooper Ressler was patrolling on his Harley Davidson on the Egg Harbor Road when a truck driver turned directly into his path. The accident left Ressler with a broken leg and a lasting memory of the dangers troopers face each day.[210]

Eventually, Ressler moved from motorcycle patrol to a desk. By 1932, the twenty-five-year-old had been assigned to state police headquarters in the teletype bureau. The state police was expanding rapidly, and monitoring of police information with teletype machines was part of that expansion.[211]

Sunday, May 1, 1932, was a dreary day, with light rain falling softy on Lakewood, New Jersey. John Ressler, in his personal vehicle—a Dodge coupe—was driving with a female passenger named Emma Burroughs. The two were heading north on Madison Avenue. At 12:40 p.m., Ressler's vehicle came to the intersection of Fourth Street and Madison. At this intersection, a truck traveling east on Fourth Street ran through the stop sign and struck the side of Ressler's car, spinning the vehicle out of control and ejecting Ressler from the car. Ressler was killed instantly. The cause of death was determined to be a broken neck.[212]

State records do not explain why Ressler was in his own car. A state police teletype reporting of the accident only states Ressler had "a girl companion" with him.[213]

LIFEGUARD

James R. Herbert #585

In 1909, Teddy Roosevelt had stepped down as president and William H. Taft was running the country. The United States' population was over ninety million, and in New Jersey, Belmar, a small community, had only three thousand residents. Located in Monmouth County, the crystal sand beaches now attract thousands of people every year. This town is significant, as it is where James Herbert was born. Born on September 1, 1909, Herbert's family lived at 710 Eighteenth Avenue in South Belmar. Herbert attended Belmar Elementary School, graduating in 1923. Afterward, he went to the regional Asbury Park High School, graduating in 1927.[214]

As a child of a beach community, it was natural that Herbert became a life guard. Many hours were spent on the beach with friends and many more swimming in the ocean; few knew this beach and the surrounding area better than James Herbert. At eighteen, Herbert was in great shape and enjoyed the social climate that came with basking in the sun as a lifeguard. During this time, Herbert was unsure what he wanted to do in life.[215]

By 1930, James was growing tired on beach patrol. Now, at twenty-one, he had matured and was looking to enter a profession that was more secure. In 1930, the stock market had made many reevaluate their occupations. Few companies were hiring, but in the midst of the economic downturn, the state police was increasing its ranks. It was an opportunity that James could not let pass. In fact, while Herbert was going through the selection process, the state police was in the news every day. In March, the child of

James Roland Herbert #585.

famed aviator Charles Lindbergh was kidnapped, which thrust the "outfit" into an international news story. The Lindbergh investigation would be scrutinized and studied by historians throughout the years. To this day, the case is controversial.[216]

For Herbert, the publicity must have added an air of excitement. In 1931, his aspirations were realized as a graduating member of the twenty-fourth class. Twenty-two troopers embarked on a new career; four of them—James Herbert #585, Francis O'Brien #592, James Scotland #594 and Warren Yenser #599—rode out on different paths leading to the same altar of public sacrifice.[217]

The twenty-one-year-old Herbert began on a motorcycle and worked out of the Berkeley Heights Barracks. When 1932 was ushered in, the "outfit" couldn't have imagined the events and heartache that would befall it. In February, Michael J. Beylon #318 was killed, and in May, John J. Ressler #494 died. Additionally, the Lindbergh kidnapping had turned into a murder investigation. The agency was under a great deal of pressure. It was during this time that Herbert was transferred to Pompton Lakes, New Jersey.[218]

Pompton Lakes station was a two-story stucco building on the Hamburg Turnpike, which runs from Paterson through several jurisdictions. It was the beginning of summer, and Herbert enjoyed thundering down the roads of Passaic County on his Harley.[219]

Two weeks after his arrival, history records Herbert riding the open roads of Wayne Township. Wayne was a large town composed mostly of farms and rural businesses, but it had its share of problems. Prohibition, and the lawlessness associated with it, stretched into rural towns like Wayne. In 1926, Charlie Ullrich #232 was gunned down in the town.[220]

The final entry in James Herbert's life came on July 9, 1932. Herbert was coming from Haledon on "Cycle No 47," roaring west on Hamburg Turnpike. It was a hot summer day, and kids from surrounding towns were being bused to a popular swimming hole in Wayne. The cold mountain water flowed down a stream into a large pond that became a popular attraction. Today, the only reminder of this pond is the stream that flows through the area.[221]

Herbert was traveling west, toward the popular pond, when he observed a speeder and was attempting to pull closer to it. Herbert came around a bend and was met with a truck in the right lane carrying kids to the swimming pond. The truck was waiting to make a left, so Herbert leaned to the left and passed the truck. In doing so, he lost control and struck an oncoming car. He was killed instantly.[222]

James Roland Herbert's funeral took place on Wednesday, July 13, at the home of his parents. Herbert was laid to rest at the Atlantic View Cemetery in Manasquan, New Jersey. He was twenty-two years old.[223]

FOG

James Scotland #594

James Scotland has a unique background. Prior to becoming a New Jersey state trooper, Scotland worked as a member of an acrobatic team and traveled extensively throughout the United States. He was a physical specimen with tremendous upper body strength. A native of Scotland, James was born in Glasgow on August 7, 1897. Historians say that Glasgow has been occupied since the prehistoric period because of its unique location near the River Clyde. Scotland's mother and father, James and Louise, had six children and lived in Glasgow during a unique time in that city's history. Many of Glasgow's architectural masterpieces were being funded and built toward the end of the nineteenth century. In 1908, the Scotlands immigrated to the United States through Canada.[224]

The Scotlands moved to Newark, New Jersey, and were a tightknit family with middle-class morals, character and values. The eleven-year-old Scotland attended the public school on Fifteenth Street.[225] James Scotland graduated grammar school in 1911, and about 1913, when he was sixteen, his parents moved to 95 Brookline Avenue in Nutley, New Jersey, a small town in Essex County. During this time, Scotland became a naturalized citizen, paving the way for his eligibility to become a law enforcement officer.[226]

After school, Scotland worked with his father as a gymnast until the United States' entry into World War I. On October 25, 1918, Scotland enlisted in the United States Coast Artillery (known today as the Coast Guard). He served at Fort Mott on the Delaware River in New Jersey. He remained

James Scotland #594 (center). *Courtesy of Virginia and Douglas Scotland.*

there for the duration of the war, being honorably discharged on February 1, 1919. He obtained the rank of bugler first class.[227]

The twenty-one-year-old resumed his vocation as an aerial gymnast, spending the next decade performing in vaudeville with his father as part of the Wilson-Aubrey Trio, which consisted of James, his father and his uncle (name unknown). They became headliners and played at the famous Palace in New York City. Furthermore, Scotland used to ride horses in the circus; however, as the years passed, and with the increasing popularity of the motion picture, vaudeville and circus acts died out.[228]

In late 1930 or early 1931, Scotland applied to the state police. He entered training as a member of the twenty-fourth class, with James Herbert #585, Warren Yenser #599 and Francis O'Brien #592. All four died in the line of duty, equating to almost 20 percent of the graduating class. This is the highest percentage of troopers killed in any one class. Interestingly, another class, the twenty-seventh, had as many troopers killed; however, this class had more troopers graduate.[229]

Scotland eventually met a woman named Anne Vanderboof, and the two wed. In April 1934, James and Anne moved to Jersey City, New Jersey. How long they were married isn't known, and their marriage bore no children.[230]

There are only glimpses into James Scotland's career. "Scottie," as his colleagues called him, assisted on the Lindbergh case and worked out of the

Flemington Barracks during the trial of Bruno Hauptmann. On Wednesday, July 9, 1932, Scotland served as a pallbearer and carried James Herbert's casket to its final resting place. Then, on August 28, 1932, three weeks after his thirty-fifth birthday, Scotland investigated a serious motor vehicle accident with such efficiency and compassion that the injured party, S.H. Conover, wrote a letter praising him:

> *What I want to bring to your personal attention is the action and bearing of Trooper Scotland on this occasion. He arrived on the scene a few minutes after the collision occurred, and, although I was dazed and little able to do anything, I could not help observing the efficiency with which Scotland handled the case. Not only was he efficient as an officer should be, but—as my wife was seriously injured—he exhibited humanity and kindness. Still, at no time did he overlook his duties as a member of your very excellent organization.*[231]

Conover concluded by describing Scotland as "efficient, substantial, and human." The next entry in Scotland's career has him driving down a foggy road.[232]

In February 1935, Scotland was working out of the Columbus Barracks, which five years prior had witnessed the strange line-of-duty death of John Divers. Now it was Thursday, February 14, and a dense fog blanketed the area of New Jersey and eastern Pennsylvania. Troopers and police officers from all over the region were busy investigating motor vehicle accidents due to the "pea soup" conditions. Trooper John Matey (see the chapter on Warren Yenser) was one of the many investigating fog-related accidents this night. Scotland and his partner, George Westervelt #433, had been in Vincentown serving a warrant and were returning back about 11:30 p.m. While driving north on the Bordentown-Columbus road (now State Highway 206) with Scotland behind the wheel, they were met with a head-on crash. The accident left Scotland in grave condition, while Westervelt and the driver of the other car had minor injuries.[233]

The next day, papers reported, "Crashes, Injuries Caused by Fog: Driving Hazardous as Blanket Covers This Section." After drastic attempts to save his life with multiple blood transfusions, James Scotland died in his hospital bed at three o'clock in the morning on Monday, February 19.[234]

Services were held at the home of his parents and the Holy Trinity Church, both in Nutley. James Scotland was laid to rest at the East Ridgelawn Cemetery in Delawanna, New Jersey. He was thirty-seven years old.[235]

ROBBERY AND MURDER

Warren G. Yenser #599

Warren Gernert Yenser was born in Lyons, Pennsylvania, on October 1, 1907. In the year of Yenser's birth, Edwin Sydney Stuart replaced Samuel Whitaker Pennypacker as governor of the state, Teddy Roosevelt was president and the small hamlet of Lyons had only five hundred residents. Lyons Borough, located in Berks County, is where Yenser's parents, John and Anna (née Rotterman), resided. They were Pennsylvania Dutch who were Protestants, and they lived an extremely modest life. They "lived [very] sparingly." It isn't known what John Yenser did for an occupation, but we do know that Anna ran a boardinghouse in Ocean Grove, New Jersey. John and Anna Yenser had five children: Warren, John, Irvin, Florence and Helen. As he grew older, Warren stayed with his mother and assisted with work duties at the boardinghouse. Eventually, Anna brought Warren to live there permanently so he could have the opportunity of attending a better school. Ocean Grove provided the perfect setting, with its streets lined with beautiful Victorian homes. It is now a beach town visited by thousands every summer. After grammar school, Warren attended Neptune's High School and played baseball and won his "letter." Academically, Yenser showed exceptional scholastic ability, graduating third in his class in 1925.[236]

After school, Yenser became an entrepreneur along with his best friend, Sheldon Engle. The two buddies opened up a shooting gallery on the boardwalk in Asbury Park, New Jersey.[237]

Warren Yenser #599.
Courtesy of Donna Dawes.

By July 1929, Warren Yenser had taken a job for the Van Ness organization in New York City. He was a sales representative for this high-powered bank firm and soon became a leading sales associate. Wall Street executives noticed the talented Pennsylvanian's performance: "W.G. Yenser…won the medal for individual bank stock sales and can truthfully be called 'Master Bank Stock Salesman'…He has headed the field since the beginning of the Triple A Bank Stock campaign, Mr. Yenser has never slackened his efforts."[238]

By the end of 1929, the twenty-one-year-old was proud of his accomplishments and was financially secure, only a few sales away from entering the prestigious "Quota Club," which only admitted "high powered sales associates." However, with the October 24 "Black Thursday" event that began the crash of the stock market, Yenser's promising career on Wall Street ended.[239]

Fate had Warren Yenser apply to the New Jersey State Police. He graduated on April 16, 1931, as a member of the twenty-fourth class.[240]

Yenser was assigned to central New Jersey and worked out of the Penn's Neck Station, where he showed the same ardent demeanor as a trooper that he had as a sales representative. He learned his job exceptionally well and became good at it. During this period, the state police was knee deep in the case of the murder/kidnapping of the Lindbergh baby. Moreover, it was constantly dealing with rumrunners, the Ku Klux Klan and other subversive groups. Yenser was a horse trooper who rode his horse Ranger. Early in his career, Yenser had stopped a man whose vehicle was unregistered. Compassionately, he let him go. The man, Joseph Mittutoheon, wrote a letter to the trooper thanking him: "I sure do appreciate and want to express my thanks many times." In the letter was a copy of the registration. Yenser was judicious, compassionate and a good judge of character.[241]

Sometime in 1934, Warren Yenser met Dorothy Blair, a beautiful brunette, who became the twinkle in his eyes. By the beginning of 1935, the two were in love and planning their wedding. Dorothy was always on his mind, as is illustrated in a note Yenser wrote on January 22, 1935: "Wonder what she is doing now…Very lonesome tonight, radio playing now, 'Night and Day you are the one,' Very true." It is evident that he was brimming with love.[242]

Four years after leaving Wall Street, the twenty-seven-year-old was doing better than most. Furthermore, his work ethic was noticed by those he served. A letter written by Iris Rose Bogorad on August 3, 1934, strikes to the heart of Yenser's magnanimous persona: "I am enclosing a money order for $2.00 to reimburse you for keeping us out of the 'hoosegow' by laying out part of our fine…We did and still do appreciate immensely your kindness in helping us out of an embarrassing situation…I must say that in doing your duty, you did it in the nicest way possible."[243]

On May 18, 1935, Warren Yenser and Dorothy Blair were wed in a ceremony at St. James Episcopal Church in Trenton. Dorothy's sister Elaine was the maid of honor and Sheldon Engle the best man. Afterward, Warren and Dorothy moved to Upper Ferry Road in Ewing Township, New Jersey. Their next-door neighbor was Hugo Stockburger #504. Stockburger had made a name for himself as one of the guards for Bruno Hauptmann, the kidnapper of Lindbergh's baby. Ewing was a quiet community close to headquarters. John Gregerson #654—the state police's first pilot—grew up there.[244]

On June 18, 1935, Yenser pulled his troop car to the side of the road and wrote four words: "Received letter from Dorothy." Later in the shift, another thought was written down: "Received phone call from Dorothy." He couldn't keep his mind off of her. He was living in the barracks, and the two spent days away from each other. In July, Dorothy became pregnant.[245]

The next entry in Yenser's life didn't come from his pen. Police pursuits are one of the most dangerous events a law enforcement officer can experience. They generally end in a limited number of ways: a crash, the perpetrator gets away or gives up and, lastly, the pursuit is terminated. In Yenser's case, the pursuit ended much differently. It was the early hours of Saturday, November 9, 1935, and Yenser was riding with John J. Matey

Sheldon Engle, Elaine Blair and Dorothy and Warren Yenser. *Courtesy of Donna Dawes.*

#384. Yenser had worked the day shift, but a trooper scheduled to work nights called out, and Yenser volunteered to take his place. About 4:30 a.m., Yenser and Matey were in the town of Sand Hill sitting on the side of the road monitoring traffic. A Chevrolet Coupe sped by, and Matey, who was driving, pulled out after the vehicle. John Matey recalled what happened: "[We] drew up alongside the vehicle and Yenser blew his whistle." The car refused to stop and accelerated. It took several miles for the troopers to catch up as the vehicles sped down the narrow highway. Matey decided to play hardball with the car and tried to push it off the road. As he pulled alongside the car, the back window burst from the sawed-off shotgun shoved through it. The muzzle erupted with the blast, hitting Yenser directly in the face and throat. Yenser fell against his partner. Spattered with blood, Matey fired back, missing his target. Enraged and determined (thinking his partner had just been killed), Matey pursued rather than render aid.[246]

The pursuit continued down into the city of Elizabeth, where the vehicle eluded Matey. Then Matey brought Yenser to Elizabeth General Hospital, where he was declared dead on arrival. As it turned out, the blast, although serious, was not fatal; the whistle Yenser had been blowing was in his mouth when the blast rang out, and he died of asphyxiation.[247]

Matey was able to get the license plate (DC-240) and determined that it was from Pennsylvania. A police bulletin went out, and Elizabeth police officers spotted the two subjects and a shootout took place. When the smoke cleared, no one had been hit. A short time later, Edward Metelski, a hardened criminal who, since the age of sixteen, had been engaged in criminality, had been captured. The other subject got away. Investigators found a sawed-off shotgun and a bottle of booze in Metelski's car. The killer refused to disclose his accomplice.[248]

On November 11, a Philadelphia landlord found the body of Albert "Whitey" Morton in an apartment. Morton was found to be the second person in the vehicle, and it was revealed that he had committed suicide by turning on the gas in his room.[249]

On Tuesday, November 12, 1935, Warren G. Yenser was buried at the Ewing Park Cemetery in Ewing Township, New Jersey. The next day, Trooper Yenser's widow, Dorothy, wrote the colonel: "I, Mrs. Dorothy E. Yenser, wife of Trooper Warren G. Yenser, do hereby make application to the New Jersey State Police Pension Fund for pension as I was solely dependant upon him for support. My father and mother who are living are unable to support me, and there is a possibility of my being pregnant."[250]

Edward Metelski was lodged in the Middlesex County Jail with a trial date set for December. Two days before his trial, he managed to escape, brandishing a handgun. One account suggests that Metelski's girlfriend provided a sexual favor to either the warden or a guard to sneak the weapon in. Nonetheless, Metelski was on the loose with another fugitive named Paul Senenko.[251]

The New Jersey State Police, which thought this horrible incident was over, was infuriated. The declaration of "get your man" that H. Norman Schwarzkopf asserted had been undermined.[252]

An undercover operation involving the state police and Newark police was initiated. Metelski's girlfriend, Mary Trianano, agreed to help the authorities bring him in. The police leaked to the paper that Trianano had not cooperated, setting the trap for Metelski to believe in Trianano's loyalty. Trianano called the fugitive and set up a meeting at a diner on Halsey Street in Newark.[253]

Yenser's next-door neighbor, Hugo Stockburger #504, was called to assist. He and other troopers took positions outside the Halsey Street location along with Newark officers. As they had thought, Metelski showed up, and after a brief struggle in which he tried to get his gun, he was taken into custody. His accomplice in the escape, Senenko, was arrested in a

Yenser is third from the left, and James Herbert #585 is sixth from the left. *Courtesy of Donna Dawes.*

restaurant a few minutes later. The state police doctrine of "get your man" was once again instituted. [254]

Edward Metelski was found guilty after a trial in which he said that Albert Morton had fired the fatal shot. The jury's verdict came after two hours of deliberation: "We find the defendant guilty of murder in the first degree, with no recommendation of mercy." Justice came swiftly, and Edward Metelski was put to the electric chair on August 4, 1936. [255]

A comforting postscript to this sad story is that Warren Yenser's daughter, Donna, was born in April 1936, and from that seed, his legacy grew. Warren Yenser has four grandchildren and seven great-grandchildren. [256]

THE MODEL TROOPER

Joseph Perry #442

Sir—They have just laid to rest…the earthly remains of Trooper Joe Perry, ofttimes called "The Model Trooper"…A young widow, and a little baby daughter, must do without the kind, stalwart, manly loved one whom they so fondly called husband and father.
—tribute written by Thomas B. Delker, editor and publisher of the
Hammonton South Jersey Star[257]

Joseph Perry was born in Larchmont, New York, on January 18, 1900. Larchmont is a small village in Westchester County that is part of the larger town of Mamaroneck on Long Island Sound. Joseph's parents, Vincent and Sadie, were of Italian heritage and had six children: Joseph, Anthony, Betty, Anglina, Nicholina and Charles. The Perry children went to Larchmont public schools. Sadie Perry died while her children were still small, leaving her husband to struggle raising their children. What Vincent Perry did for a living isn't known.[258]

In 1917, at age seventeen, Perry enlisted in the United States Army and was attached to the Sixteenth Infantry and shipped overseas. As a foot soldier during the First World War, he experienced much action and was awarded the Silver Star for valor, the Bronze Star for bravery and a Distinguished Service Medal for his notable service. Moreover, he received the Purple Heart after he was wounded. When the war concluded in 1919, Perry remained in the military until he was twenty-nine years old.[259]

Joseph Perry #442.

The decorated war hero applied to the New Jersey State Police, and before long, he was doing push-ups and sit-ups at the state police academy. On July 1, 1929, as a member of the twentieth class, Joseph Perry was sworn in and assigned to Troop B.[260]

Perry worked out of the Flemington Station and, while there, served as Richard Hauptmann's guard during the Lindbergh trial. A noteworthy achievement for Perry was when he and trooper Louis C. Marshall #406 attempted to save the life of a man who had been consumed by acid fumes. The two troopers responded to a call to a vinegar plant where a worker had fallen into a vat of acid. Marshall grabbed a rope and tied it around himself, and Perry lowered him into the vat. The acid fumes enveloped Marshall, and he fell unconscious. Perry pulled both men out of the vat. The worker had succumbed to the vapor, and Perry resuscitated Marshall, who was near death. For his efforts, Perry was awarded a lifesaving medal. On June 9, 1931, Perry was assigned to south Jersey (Troop A).[261]

About 1933 or 1934, Joseph Perry met Mildred "Millie" Nicoli at a community dance, and soon they were in love. Perry, while on mounted patrol in Port Norris, would ride his horse over to the Nicoli farm to visit his love. He made so many treks that his horse would head to the farm unguided.

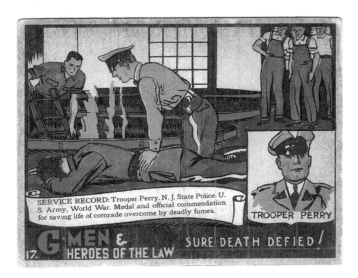

Cartoon of Perry's lifesaving. *Courtesy of Barbara Adams*.

Francis O'Brien #592 was transferred into the area and received Perry's horse, and he soon found his new horse bringing him over to the Nicoli farm as well. O'Brien and Perry were friends and had worked together at Port Norris. Sadly, a few years later, O'Brien would also die in the line of duty.[262]

In 1934, Joseph and Millie wed and moved to Vineland, New Jersey, where they bought a house on the corner of Main Street and Fairmount Avenue. Joseph and Millie, according to their family, were a "love match." In July 1935, their daughter Barbara was born. The couple had the ideal home.[263]

The final chapter of Joseph Perry's life was written on June 7, 1937, a crisp Monday morning. About 10:00 a.m., Perry, riding motorcycle #2, was on patrol in the farmland community of Centerton in Salem County. By 1937, ten Jersey troopers had perished on motorcycles. As Perry turned onto the Elmer-Centerton road, he was about to be the eleventh.[264]

Schalick's Feed Farm was a popular mill where local farmers came for supplies. Located on the western side of the road, Schalick's had been busy with customers for hours by the time Perry was idling by. James Brady, an eighty-two-year-old, had made a few purchases, and without looking, he drove his Ford sedan out of the parking lot and directly into the path of Joe Perry. Perry was sent flying through the air and landed fifteen feet away on the macadam roadway.[265]

Trooper Perry was rushed to Newcomb Hospital, where doctors treated him for a compound fracture of both bones in his right leg. He also had a considerable portion of flesh torn from one of those legs. The thirty-seven-year-old slipped

Joseph, Millie and Barbara. *Courtesy of Barbara Adams.*

into a coma when additional complications manifested. A gas bacillus infection set in stemming from his fractures, and massive doses of polyvalent serum were administered to combat the infection. According to doctors, a "very virulent poisoning of the system" caused his demise, a condition that is rather rare but not unheard of. Millie was at his side when he passed away.[266]

Joseph Perry was buried on Friday, June 11, and was laid to rest at Sacred Heart Cemetery on Walnut Road in Vineland, New Jersey.[267]

Seventy years later, in December 2007, Millie Perry lay dying in bed grasping a photo of herself and Joseph. One of the last things Millie said was, "Oh how I love my Perry." She never remarried.[268]

STRUGGLE FOR A STRONG MAN

Matthew Francis McManus #144

Life begins at forty.[269]

T he story of Matthew McManus is a sorrowful tale that begins with his birth on May 3, 1898, in the city of Newark to Francis and Mary, who were devout Catholic parents. Francis McManus's vocation isn't known, and he died when Matthew was just a boy. Matthew attended St. James Catholic School in Newark and it is there he received his sole education.[270]

From age fourteen until nineteen, nothing is recorded of Matthew McManus's life. Records indicate that on Saturday, January 2, 1915, he began working for the Hercules Powder Company in Kenvil, New Jersey. The company manufactured explosives used for mining and the military. Two years later, on September 19, 1917, McManus entered the army. The world was at war, and McManus was going to play a role, no matter how small.[271] Matthew, or "Mac," as friends and family called him, became a member of the First Air Service regiment, Special Casual Company No. 2922. He rose through the ranks and became a sergeant. Whether he experienced combat isn't known. He was honorably discharged upon the close of the war.[272]

At the age of twenty-four, Mac began working as an automobile mechanic, eventually rising to foreman. However, shortly after his promotion, he moved

Matthew Francis McManus #144. *Courtesy of Ann McManus.*

U.S. Army. *Courtesy of Ann McManus.*

to Arizona. What sparked this sojourn isn't certain. In October 1921, while he was planning his Arizona trek, members of the first state police class were training for their December graduation. While in the desert, McManus worked for the Copper Company of Arizona.[273] His stay in Arizona didn't work out, and he returned to the Garden State, where he took up a position as a pipe fitter for the Standard Oil Company.[274]

By age twenty-six, McManus had moved to Morristown, New Jersey, a quaint community nestled in the hills of Morris County. Morristown is renowned as the place where George Washington headquartered during

McManus in Arizona (note the dog on the car). *Courtesy of Ann McManus.*

the Revolutionary War. While McManus lived there, he became friendly with many local business owners, some of whom vouched for him when he applied to the state police.[275]

At only 146 pounds and standing five feet, seven inches, he may not have been tall in stature, but he stood tall in strength and fortitude. In the academy, McManus performed slightly above average. On Saturday, April 1, 1922, McManus, with forty-one other men, became a Jersey trooper. His first assignment was Netcong Station in Troop B.[276]

On Sunday, July 16, 1922, while on patrol in Hackettstown, McManus stopped his Harley on Mill Street near the Musconetcong River. His reasons for doing so aren't clear; possibly he was watching the waters of the Musconetcong flow past this section of road. A newspaper account states that McManus was standing alongside his motorcycle. It is possible that he was just enjoying the day and the natural beauty of the river. Upon mounting his cycle, he kick-started the motor and inattentively turned into the road in front of an oncoming car. The impact threw McManus and marked the first motorcycle accident that would claim the life of a New Jersey state trooper. However, it took sixteen years to claim his life.[277]

McManus was transported to Dover General Hospital, where doctors performed emergency surgery on him. He had a ruptured Jejunum (the second portion of his small intestine). The impact completely severed his intestine, leaving him in the hospital for a whole month. While in the hospital, he developed Bradycardia, which is a condition where the heart rate is reduced.[278]

The next year would be difficult for the young trooper, as he had several operations for various ailments stemming from the accident. His physician, Dr. Mills, recorded these events: "I operated upon him for appendicitis, adhesions and the hernia. I have seen him a number of times in the attacks of Bradycardia, and I believe that this is due to the effects of the original accident."[279] On May 3, 1924, McManus celebrated his twenty-sixth birthday, and later that month his pain and discomfort led to an operation to remove his left testicle.[280]

By late June, McManus was back on patrol. He was working the day Trooper Robert Coyle #238 was gunned down. While helping to comb the area looking for the "murder car," he and Sergeant William J. Ryan #81 spotted a vehicle that they believed to be connected to the murder. The car was stopped, and the four occupants were asked to step out of the vehicle. In doing so, two pulled guns on the troopers, with one pressing a gun into McManus's ribcage. Mac remained calm and simply told the man he had made a mistake. The man lowered his weapon, and they hopped in their car and sped away. The two troopers pursued and forced the car off the road. The gunmen were captured, but the other two suspects escaped.[281]

In 1925, several medical problems from his accident began to worsen, and throughout the year, McManus was in and out of the hospital. Then, the following year, he was gravely assaulted in the French Hill speakeasy undercover operation. While recovering from these injuries, Anna Geary was assigned as his hospital nurse. Anna came from a large family and had been practicing nursing since the age of sixteen. The two fell in love and married.[282]

McManus returned to duty, but it wasn't long before he realized that he could no longer enforce the law. On March 5, 1927, McManus sat at a typewriter and wrote to Colonel Schwarzkopf: "Dear Sir, Finding that it is impossible for me to perform the duties of a Trooper, due to injuries received in a accident while on motorcycle patrol, on the Netcong Hackettstown road on July 16, 1922, I respectfully request to be relieved from duty and be placed under the pension act of The N.J. State Police."[283]

On April 1, 1927, Matthew McManus's tenure with the state police came to an end. For the next twelve years, Mac was in and out of the hospital for an array of health issues, some stemming from his motorcycle accident and others from his assault. In May of that year, Anna and Matthew had their first child, a daughter named Ann.[284]

By 1930, they were living in Stanhope and had a two-bedroom home on the main thoroughfare. McManus worked odd jobs to supplement his pension, including one venture operating a diner from an old trolley car. As a father, McManus loved his little daughter and took her everywhere. They went fishing and even pistol shooting together. "He was a very good father," Ann remembers. "Every morning I had to eat my breakfast…and I had to put my school clothes out every night and polish my shoes." She laughs, "If I didn't finish the plate, it would be there the next morning." McManus also had a passion for dogs. If he saw a stray, he would take it home. There were dogs all over the McManus property. His daughter remembers all the dogs and how he used to line fish up on a string after fishing. "He also taught me to shoot a gun. We used to line up cans and shoot at them…he was so good to me," says Ann. One of the things his daughter remembers her father saying was, "Life begins at forty." In 1932, Matthew and Anna had their second child, a son named John.[285]

For the next eight years, McManus struggled with his illness but made the most of his time with his wife and children. Then, on January 17, 1938, he had sharp pains in his stomach and was hospitalized. Three days later, his condition worsened. Dr. Mills recorded his findings: "Mr. McManus is in grave condition and will have to remain in the hospital for a long period of time. All of these various conditions are due to the motorcycle accident that he had."[286]

On February 28, 1938, McManus succumbed to the injuries that he had sustained on that summer day in 1922.[287]

LONG RIDE

Vincent C. Vosbein # 633

Vincent Vosbein was a young man who saw his dreams of becoming a trooper come to fruition as a graduating member of the twenty-sixth class. His picture hangs in the state police museum and is displayed at various troop headquarters spread throughout New Jersey. But who is the man in the picture?[288]

Vincent C. Vosbein was born on June 8, 1913, in Manahawken, New Jersey. His parents, Viggo and Anna, had three children, with Vincent being their only son. The Vosbeins lived in Jersey City, and Vincent and his sisters grew up playing in the city streets. Jersey City sits on the west bank of the Hudson River across from lower Manhattan, and it was a community of blue-collar workers, mainly dock workers. In fact, Jersey City had more people living there in 1913 than it does today.[289]

Vosbein briefly attended high school in Summit but returned to Jersey City, where he attended the Dickinson High School. Records do not indicate what Vosbein did after graduating.[290]

In May 1935, a month before his twenty-second birthday, Vosbein joined the National Guard, serving with the 107th Infantry in New York. The 107th Infantry is rich in history and had seen combat on a number of occasions, dating back to the Civil War. The guard emphasized the effectiveness of training, discipline and strength of character, virtues that served Vosbein well.[291]

By 1937, Schwarzkopf's vision for his "outfit" had brought the agency to the forefront in law enforcement. However, times were changing, as Mark

Vincent C. Vosbein #633.

O. Kimberling took over as superintendent after Schwarzkopf left under a cloud of doubt and disappointment over the Lindbergh case. As Vosbein was going through the selection process for the state police, Superintendent Kimberling wrote him:

> *My dear Mr. Vosbein…it is noted that you are now 23 years of age, but that you will be 24 on June 8th. We are willing to give you an opportunity of going into training with this class on June 1st, provided you do so with the understanding that it will be impossible to compensate you for the period of June 1st to June 8th, inclusive, and that the rate of compensation for the month of June, in the event you remain with us that long, would only be from June 9th to June 30th. Of course, thereafter you will be paid accordingly on the basis the others receive compensation.*[292]

One has to be a trooper to understand the joy Vosbein felt when he got that letter. Fortunately, Kimberling was progressive and realized that Vosbein was a valuable applicant, one whom he didn't want to lose on a technicality. On June 1, 1937, Vosbein, along with fifteen others, became a New Jersey state trooper.[293]

Trooper Vosbein began his career on a Harley Davidson and, by the summer of 1938, was wrapping up his first year. It was a transition for him; no longer did he have the freedom he had once enjoyed. Now, he was part of a quasi-military organization, with permission needed for just about everything.[294]

The cold weather ushered in 1938, and Vosbein found himself transferred to the Somerville Station, a two-story stone structure that is still in operation today. It is a facility rich in state police history. Prior to Vosbein, Bob Coyle and "Big" Mike Beylon walked the corridors of this building.[295]

Vincent Vosbein celebrated his twenty-fifth birthday on Wednesday, June 8, with the events of the day going unrecorded. This would be his last birthday.[296]

Nine days after cutting his birthday cake, Vosbein mounted his Harley Davidson at Somerville and drove out into state police history. The date was Friday, June 17, 1938.[297] It was a pleasant day, and late in the afternoon, Vosbein pulled up to a roadside stand, where he talked with the proprietor for a while. Afterward, he hopped back on his bike and headed down the road.[298]

Vosbein was traveling south and came to the Somerville Circle, where he rounded the road and proceeded south on Route 31 (today, Route 202). As Vosbein approached the intersection with Frelinghuysen Avenue, a small truck turned sharply to its left directly in front of Vosbein. According to a witness, the truck turned so quickly that it was impossible for the trooper to react. Witnesses stated that Vosbein's motorcycle spun around three times, throwing the trooper facedown onto the roaz   d.[299]

At the hospital, Vosbein's condition worsened with each passing day. Blood was found in his spinal fluid, and an examination revealed a laceration to the brain. A brain surgeon was brought in; however, all efforts to save the young man were futile. Vincent Vosbein died on June 19.[300]

Coincidentally, the state police message number announcing Vosbein's death, #633, was the same as his badge number. Hundreds of people gathered on Wednesday, June 22, at the funeral parlor in Barnegat, New Jersey. A tearful service, attended by family, friends and hundreds of complete strangers, followed the hearse to the Greenwood Cemetery in Tuckerton, New Jersey.[301]

ICE AND THE JENNY JUMP

Walter B. Otte #668

Walter Bertrand Otte was born on Sunday, June 7, 1908, to William and Mary Otte. Walter's father was of German heritage, whereas Mary (née McCommell) was Irish. William lived in West Hoboken, which consisted mostly of German immigrants, most of whom spoke their native tongue. Mary lived in nearby Union Hill, and like the couple, West Hoboken and Union Hill joined and became Union City in 1925. The couple initially had two children, both of whom died young. Their heartache was unimaginable but lessened a little with the birth of Walter. The couple lived at 526 Deebois Street and went on to have two other children, Mildreth and Margaret.[302]

Otte attended Emerson High School on Eighteenth Street in town and played football in the mid-1920s during the "leather helmet" era. Family members describe Otte as a "rough and ready" kid who grew up on the streets of Hudson County. His mother and father owned a diner on New York Avenue in Union City, and Otte spent much of his youth hanging around with siblings and their circle of friends from Jersey City heights.[303]

Otte was crazy about motorcycles, and while in high school he would travel to Hoboken, which was still undeveloped and provided plenty of open space for racing. On one of these events, Otte was seriously injured in a mishap. Looking back, family members believe that this was a foreshadowing of what was to come.[304]

Walter Bertrand Otte #668.

In 1926, Otte was accepted into Hobart College in Geneva, New York, a liberal arts college that sits on 188 acres on the shore of beautiful Lake Seneca. He studied here for two years and then left to pursue a career as a trade broker. At the age of twenty, Otte was working on Wall Street. This same year, he and his parents moved to Secaucus.[305]

During the Depression, Walter left Wall Street and worked at an Esso gas station in Secaucus, near his parents' home. Walter always enjoyed working on cars and repairing motorcycles. Working here gave the young man the idea of getting a job where he could get paid for what he liked to do. As such, he filled out a state police application. It is presumed that during this period he met and wed his wife, Anne.[306]

At the age of thirty, Walter Otte became a graduating member of the twenty-seventh state police class. Fifty-five members entered training in August 1938, but only forty-seven graduated; of these were John Gregerson #654, Frank Trainor #682 and Joseph Walter #685, all of whom lost their lives at the altar of public service. The twenty-seventh and twenty-fourth classes have the most troopers who died in the line of duty.[307]

Walter Otte was transferred to Troop B and assigned to the Flemington Sub-Station as a motorcycle trooper. On Monday, January 2, 1939, at about 4:00 p.m., Otte was in Clinton Township riding down Route 28 and was involved in a motorcycle accident that fractured his jaw and nose and caused several of his teeth to be knocked out. He spent a month in Somerset Hospital. Family members say that Otte was an excellent rider but handled a motorcycle aggressively. [308]

By January 1940, Otte was working at the Blairstown Barracks in rural Warren County. Like Flemington's area, Blairstown served as an agrarian community. To this day, there is little industry in this region. Troopers here are responsible for policing the small towns that spread throughout the county.[309]

If the year 1939 could be looked at as being kind to Otte, the year 1940 could be called unforgiving. January is normally bitter cold in the Garden State, and the morning of Wednesday, January 24, 1940, was no different. The temperature was about thirty degrees, and Otte was on patrol with his Harley Davidson. He had stopped at troop headquarters in Morristown and then headed back to Blairstown. At 11:00 a.m., Otte stopped in Hackettstown and got a haircut. Afterward, he throttled down Old Vienna Road (Route 46) and turned right onto Great Meadows–Hope Road (known today as County Road 611/Hope Road). It was about 11:45 a.m. when he made that right turn.[310]

Great Meadows–Hope Road is an isolated thoroughfare that cuts through the Jenny Jump Mountain and provides a scenic view of the valley at the peak. At this point of the road, there exist two distinct bends. Up until this point the road had been clear; however, near this section water running off the mountain was seeping out onto the road and turning to ice, eventually creating a sheet of ice that extended two feet onto the roadway. Presumably, Otte didn't notice this hazard. He drove right onto the ice and lost control. His front wheel then got caught in a drainage ditch. Otte tried to maintain his balance by dragging his left boot on the pavement but was unable to keep control and was thrown facedown onto the pavement until he came to a rest on a small slope on the side of the road.[311]

At 12:00 p.m., a passing motorist noticed the fallen trooper facedown and groaning. The concerned citizen took Otte and drove him to Dr. Storm, a local physician in Hope Township. From Storm's office, Otte was transported to Newton Hospital.[312]

Every effort was made to save his life, but all were in vain. At 2:34 p.m., Walter Otte died. An hour later, the state police teletype transmission went out: "Trooper Walter Bertrand Otte, NJ State Police stationed at Blairstown,

NJ was killed in a motorcycle accident this afternoon. The cause of death was determined to be a severe skull fracture."[313]

On Saturday, January 27, funeral services were held at the parlor of John Leber at 4070 Boulevard and Twentieth Street in Union City, New Jersey. Otte was laid to rest in the Holy Name Cemetery on Westside Avenue in Jersey City, New Jersey.[314]

AVIATION

John I. Gregerson #654

H istoric Trenton brings thoughts of the American Revolution, with
George Washington riding into town with his Continental army to
capture Hessian soldiers in a daring raid. Further reflection brings about
thoughts of the state's capital and the leaders who have served there. And, a
little-known fact, one of historical importance to the "outfit," is that on July
12, 1912, Daisy Gregerson gave birth to her first son, John Ivins Gregerson,
here in the city. Gregerson was the first pilot in the organization and, sadly,
the only trooper to die from a duty-related aviation crash.[315]

Morton and Daisy Gregerson lived in the nearby town of Ewing at 1651
Pennington Road. The Gregersons had another son named David a few
years later. The Gregerson children went to William Lanning Elementary
School in Ewing. Young John Gregerson was a fresh-faced, free-spirited kid
who, while strolling to school, used to gaze up and watch the high-flying
airplane that took off from a farm off Bear Tavern Road. "Old" Alfred
Reeder owned the property and had an airplane landing strip. It was an
amazing sight high above the road. It was the early twentieth century, and
plane flight was still a marvel to watch, especially for a young boy.[316]

Gregerson was an ambitious kid, and at the age of fourteen, he registered
with the Boy Scouts, Troop 15 in Ewing, which had just been formed. In fact,
he was one of the first to enroll. Troop 15 is one of the oldest in the state.[317]

By 1926, Gregerson was attending the regional Trenton High School.
This was a significant year for him, as it was the year he had his first flying

John Ivins Gregerson #654.

lesson. No longer would the fresh-faced kid just stare up at the sky. One can only imagine the excitement he must have felt. By 1929, Reeder's farm had evolved into a small airport called Skillman Airport. As Gregerson flew over the green pastures surrounding Ewing, one wonders if he thought of his future and the role flying would have in it.[318]

After school, Gregerson continued his lessons and, to support his passion, worked various jobs throughout the area. One such job was as a milkman for the Oakland Dairy in West Trenton. In October 1934, the twenty-two-year-old worked as a salesman for the Brenfleck Coal Company. Throughout his twenties, Gregerson acquired many hours of flight time, and after working three years as a salesman, he decided to parlay his flying skills into an occupation.[319]

On Monday, August 15, 1938, John Gregerson entered training with the state police and ultimately graduated as a member of the twenty-seventh class. Notable graduates were Walter Otte, Frank Trainor and Joseph Walter Jr., all of whom died while wearing the uniform of a Jersey trooper.[320]

It didn't take the "outfit" long to realize Gregerson's unique skills and detach him to the Department of Aviation. John Gregerson was the sole representative in aviation for the state police.[321] Aviation was experiencing rapid growth, and New Jersey witnessed several significant aviational events: the world's largest passenger plane was built in Teterboro, and Amelia Earhart prepared for her first transatlantic flight there. Sadly, the most tragic of these events happened in the sky over Lakehurst when the Hindenburg exploded. Throughout history, exploration has always come with a price.

On Friday, April 28, 1939, Gregerson reported to the Department of Aviation and worked there throughout the summer. This gave him the opportunity to work with seasoned pilots. For Gregerson, this proved to be a period of growth. In September, Gregerson was back to patrol. The superintendent knew that aviation would have an intricate part in policing, and Trooper Gregerson would be the lead player for the organization.[322]

The winter of 1939 witnessed Gregerson patrolling the rural towns of Troop C out of the Farmindale Barracks.[323]

The year 1940 ushered in the third decade for the state police and witnessed the economy beginning to prosper as the Great Depression faded into history. The fundamental reason for this growth was the preparations the United States was making for possible war. Gregerson was entering his second year as a trooper, and his skills were becoming more refined. Gregerson knew that to be an asset in the air, he needed to be one on the ground.[324]

Civil aviation had become a concern for state officials as more and more airplanes filled the skies and the threat of war lingered in the air. A defense program within New Jersey had been developed, and in early November 1940, the aviation commissioner requested Gregerson. The timing was perfect, for early in 1941, a Civil Air Patrol was formed.[325]

Gregerson pooled his money with his friend Miller Engemann and bought an airplane. At this time in his life, another passion took hold. He began participating in sharpshooting competitions and became friendly with a local gunsmith named Ernest Baldwin. Together, they practiced long hours. Gregerson spent many hours at Baldwin's home at 2 Woodbury Road in Trenton, and Baldwin's son William remembers these social gatherings well: "He used to come over to our house almost every weekend." Gregerson used to tell trooper stories, especially those centering on his aerial duties. Gregerson flew over the Jersey Pine Barrens looking for illegal activity such as bootleggers and rumrunners. However, the most impressionable moment for William was when Gregerson took the then nine-year-old up in his airplane. "I remember flying in that plane," says Baldwin. "It is the only time I ever flown in a plane when I was a kid."[326]

When spring came, Gregerson took advantage of the optimal flying conditions and spent more time in the cockpit. On Wednesday, April 16,

1941, at about 5:30 p.m., Gregerson headed over to the Mercer Airport for a flying lesson. He arrived at 6:00 p.m. and met with his instructor. After running through a preflight list, the radio tower cleared the two for takeoff. According to the account, wheels went up for Gregerson at 6:45 p.m. His lift was gradual at first, but for reasons unknown, Gregerson increased his lift too quickly and caused the engine to stall. The plane turned sharply and nose-dived to the ground, falling three hundred feet. The impact broke both of Gregerson's legs and his arm, and he had serious head trauma. His instructor miraculously received only minor injuries.[327]

In a letter to Colonel Kimberling, Gill Robb Wilson, the director of aviation, said that the plane's quick descent was too much for Gregerson's experience. He "was a fair pilot…[but] had [a] limited amount of time" flying. Interestingly, Wilson states that Gregerson was not working at the time of the crash. And though this was true, Wilson wrote, "The point I wish to make clear is that this trooper was highly a conscientious man who met his death during an activity which would more completely fit him for his job as a trooper."[328]

Two weeks after this horrible crash, on Monday, April 28, the twenty-eight-year-old New Jersey state trooper succumbed to his injuries.[329]

After Gregerson's death, Director Wilson wrote, "He was not an idle boy fooling around for a little pleasure…[he] was a young man of the highest type, capable, conscientious and enthusiastic." Wilson continued, "I know you will add his name to that roll of fine boys who have died in the service of the state, so many of whom I have known and admired. Gregerson was a fine trooper, proud and loyal of his outfit and his service to New Jersey."[330]

Full police honors were bestowed upon him at his funeral. John Gregerson was buried at the Greenwood Cemetery on Greenwood Avenue in Hamilton Township, New Jersey.[331]

THE FRUIT STAND

William J. Doolan #824

Williiam Joseph Doolan was born in Bayonne, New Jersey, on Wednesday, September 3, 1913, to Timothy Doolan and his wife. Like Cornelious O'Donnell before and Joseph Wirth after, Doolan was raised in the city of Bayonne. Bayonne sits across from Staten Island, New York, and is a peninsula surrounded by New York Bay, Newark Bay and the Kill van Kull River. Doolan was educated in the public school system through high school. Afterward, he enrolled in Drake's Business College, which offered studies in a variety of trades. The institute is where skills can be acquired in less than two years; Doolan completed his course of study in one.[332]

Afterward, Doolan worked for the City of Bayonne as a salvage worker. Also at this time, the nineteen-year-old joined the New Jersey National Guard. Nothing is known of Doolan from age nineteen until his entry into the New Jersey State Police at the age of twenty-nine.[333] Doolan became a trooper as a graduating member of the thirty-first class on October 15, 1942. He was assigned to Troop B.[334]

The 1940s were a time of growth, both in skills and size, for the state police. During the first two decades, the "outfit" lost twenty troopers. This period also witnessed Schwarzkopf retire under the political fallout from the Lindbergh investigation. World events caused the United States to drastically increase its preparation for war, and a civil defense program in New Jersey was formed. The state police kept producing classes because of the increasing role the organization had in state affairs.[335]

William Joseph Doolan #824.

From October 1942 until October 1944, Doolan served at several locations throughout Troop B. He was a trooper during a time of uncertainty and angst as citizens lived in fear after the attack on Pearl Harbor in December 1941. The possibility of war on the homeland was very real. Law enforcement across the country was on the lookout for terrorist activity. The generation of 9/11, with the attacks on the World Trade Center and the Pentagon, can relate to Doolan's generation, for the pulse of the nation was much the same then as it was in 2001. In 1941, troopers could be seen guarding factories, bridges, businesses and other important facilities. It is during this environment that the third superintendent, Colonel Charles H. Schoeffel, was sworn in.[336]

It is believed that during this period, Doolan met and married a woman named Verena (last name unknown). Records indicate that William and Verena Doolan purchased a home at 741 Kennedy Boulevard in Bayonne, New Jersey.[337]

Records of October 21, 1944, have William Doolan working out of the Ramsey Station and getting off duty at 5:20 p.m. Doolan said goodbye to Trooper Charles Kiseljack #477 and walked out the door. Kiseljack, working the "station record," recorded that Doolan was out on "night pass and one week vacation." Each facility keeps a station record (ledger) that records the events of the day. The person assigned to the book (trooper parlance) is normally a sergeant, but in this case the sergeant was off. Doolan was clearly off duty when he died, but for reasons not known, he is listed as dying in the line of duty. As such, the following narrative depicts the event that took his life.[338]

Over two hours after being logged out of the station, Doolan drove his personal vehicle into the parking lot of the J.O. fruit stand off Highway 17 in Lodi, New Jersey. Doolan purchased several items and then left. The thirteen-year-old cashier was impressed by the slender, well-built man with a serious expression and Hitler-like mustache, and she watched him walk to his car. A moment later, the sound of two vehicles impacting was heard.[339]

What happened is that Doolan turned north, crossing the southbound lanes, and was hit by an oncoming car. He was rushed to the Hackensack Hospital, and for two days, doctors desperately tried to save his life. Blood donations were requested, with the only matching donor type being Clifford Bebout #638.[340]

On October 23, 1944, William Doolan went into cardiac arrest and died at 6:20 a.m. with a trooper guard at his side.[341] He was buried at the Holy Cross Cemetery in North Arlington, New Jersey.[342]

WHERE OTHERS WOULD NOT GO

Francis R. O'Brien #592

Francis Robert O'Brien was born on February 6, 1909, in Nutley, New Jersey. O'Brien's childhood is hard to decipher, but it is known that he attended school in Newark from first grade through third. Thereafter, the family moved to Spring Lake, New Jersey, and lived at 312 Pitney Avenue. They purchased several homes on this street. According to the O'Brien family, Jeremiah O'Brien (Francis's father) invented the towel rack that is commonly used in bathrooms. The Scott Company bought the patent, and this is where Mary and Jeremiah gained their financial success. The O'Briens had a large family, beginning with Francis, followed by Ann, Raymond, Margaret, Mary and Arthur.[343]

The O'Briens provided their children with the finest education possible. Francis was educated at Norwood Military Academy in Philadelphia, Pennsylvania. Norwood was a strict military structured school, and it is here that he developed the principles that would stay with him throughout his life.[344]

By the age of eighteen, O'Brien stood five feet, ten inches, weighed 160 pounds and had brown hair with blue eyes. He was studying electrical engineering during the day and working as a driver in Asbury Park at night. It is around this time that his father, Jeremiah, became ill and required much

Francis Robert O'Brien #592. *Courtesy of Francis W. O'Brien.*

care. During this crisis, O'Brien's mother and siblings became dependent upon him for emotional support. Jeremiah's illness was long and drawn out, draining the O'Brien money.[345]

This was a difficult time within the O'Brien home; they lost a father and their money during the period known as the Great Depression. O'Brien had to drop out of school to support his family. He then performed an act that would change his life. He applied to the New Jersey State Police for employment.[346]

O'Brien trained as a member of the twenty-fourth class along with James Scotland #594, Warren Yenser #599 and James Herbert #585. As a state trooper, O'Brien witnessed a period, beginning in July 1932 and ending in November 1935, during which Scotland, Yenser and Herbert were killed in the line of duty. It was a difficult time for the alumni of the twenty-fourth class.[347]

Trooper O'Brien bore badge #592 and was stationed out of south Jersey. In 1931, the page of history records O'Brien working out of the Port Norris Station. While there, the twenty-two-year-old met Beatrice Conahey. Port Norris had five to six hundred residents at the time and was the world's largest oyster center. Beatrice's father was an oysterman who had a thriving business. On May 2, 1933, Francis and Beatrice wed.[348]

State police records speak of O'Brien's heroism, bravery and bravado. On August 6, 1935, O'Brien grabbed the handlebars of his Harley and throttled out of the state police lot. A Jersey trooper with his unique uniform has an air of authority with a lingering aroma of awe. While riding through the town of Millville in Cumberland County, O'Brien saw a bright light torching the night sky. The motorcycle cop realized the light was that of a house fire. The house was the home of Benjamin Salter and his wife; they resided on Bridgeton Pike Road and had a small child.[349]

As O'Brien roared up to the home, scores of people filled the street. Firemen and good Samaritans placed ladders on the house and were trying to break through windows to save the young child still inside. With each attempt, the men were forced back by intense heat from the flames.[350]

O'Brien heeled his kickstand down and dismounted. Once told of the infant trapped in the home, he knew he had to do something. The firemen were having no success, so O'Brien unbuckled his gun belt and let it drop to the ground. He was going in! O'Brien had the firemen hose him down with water, and then he climbed the ladder. Inside, while looking for the infant, the floor gave way, and O'Brien fell almost completely through to the room below. He pulled himself up and found the child. Wrapping the child in a wet towel, he carried the infant outside. The child was rushed to the hospital, but efforts to save the infant's life were unsuccessful. O'Brien had to be treated for smoke inhalation.[351]

In October 1935, Francis and Beatrice celebrated the birth of their only child, a son, Francis William O'Brien.[352]

For his daring entry, the New Jersey State Police conferred upon Francis O'Brien the Merit Award for Outstanding Bravery. Brave he was. There was also a compassionate side to the man, as Mr. Joseph Missley, an attorney from Harrisburg, Pennsylvania, attested:

On July 25, 1936…my car was struck by another automobile and completely demolished…I wish to site for your approval the conduct of

Francis, Beatrice and little Francis. *Courtesy of Francis W. O'Brien.*

Trooper...O'Brien, who after seeing all of the persons safely on the way to the hospital who had been injured, himself visited the hospital and there reassured us regarding the accident. He then...secured transportation for the other members of our party to the point of destination.[353]

Francis Robert O'Brien was a unique man; some would say he was a trooper's trooper. Missley wrote that "O'Brien stood out as the acme of courtesy, and efficiency." Unfortunately, his heroic efforts in August 1935 caused more damage to his lungs than had been expected. O'Brien began to suffer intermittent hemorrhages. The damage from the smoke had left his lungs vulnerable and his immune system frail. Somewhere along the way, O'Brien's weakened lungs were exposed to tuberculosis.[354]

On April 21, 1939, a medical examination of O'Brien revealed that he had contracted tuberculosis. On May 4, O'Brien was admitted to the New Jersey Sanatorium for Tuberculosis Diseases. O'Brien would spend the next two years here. In the beginning of 1941, he was told that he had severe cavities on his lungs and surgery was not an option. Doctors recommended that he try a change of environment combined with strict bed rest in the hope that some clearing of his lungs would occur. In March 1941, O'Brien resigned from the state police. Major Mark O. Kimberling wrote to the State House Commission describing O'Brien's diagnoses: "He [O'Brien] has reached the maximum of his gain with his Institution, that the future does not look too good…a contributing factor to this man's condition may be traced to the fact that, under date of August 6, 1935…[he] suffered from the effects of inhalation of smoke."[355]

For the remainder of his life, O'Brien was in and out of the hospital. It was difficult on his wife raising their child alone. The next four years witnessed

Deputy sheriff. *Courtesy of Francis W. O'Brien.*

O'Brien struggling to beat his illness in Tucson, Arizona. They lived in a trailer and then moved to an apartment and finally rented a house. The climate appeared to agree with O'Brien; his breathing became easier and his health improved. To augment his pension, O'Brien became a deputy sheriff. For a time, everything appeared to be going well for the young couple. As time went on, Beatrice began to become homesick for her family, and her loving husband acquiesced and moved his family back to New Jersey.[356]

By the spring of 1944, the O'Briens had moved in with relatives. They remained there for six months until Francis and Beatrice found a home in High Bridge. Only a week after moving into their new home, in the early morning hours of November 27, 1944, Francis Robert O'Brien passed away. The cause of death was listed as "a hemorrhage caused by a lung infection."[357]

Beatrice O'Brien worked four jobs a day to support herself and Francis William. When Francis William was old enough, he left high school to support his mother. He went on to become a New Jersey state trooper like his dad, badge number 1653. Francis William had two sons, Kevin and Keith, both of whom entered law enforcement: Kevin became a trooper in January 1986, and Keith is a Millville police officer. Keith patrols the same city where his grandfather entered a burning building during the summer of 1935.[358]

AXE KILLING AND THE SHOOTING OF A TROOPER

Cornelius A. O'Donnell #367

Sergeant C. O'Donnell was a beloved man, not just by friends and relatives but also by the communities he served. When residents learned that O'Donnell was being transferred, a storm of letters flooded Colonel Schwarzkopf's office. The editor of the *Paterson Evening News* wrote, "We, on the *News* have had contact with the State Police at Pompton Lakes for many years…I feel frank to say that no combination of officers has been so cooperative and so universally popular in this territory." Green was speaking about O'Donnell's relationship with the Pompton Lakes Station commander, Sergeant John Doyle #287. Together, they provided a service that many police chiefs could only hope to achieve. The local pastor, Reverend Philip McCool, wrote, "We trust that you will not consider the following request forward or meddlesome…[O'Donnell's] influence as a model Trooper, a kind, wholesome, principled Christian gentleman cannot easily be dispensed with." These declarations speak volumes of a man who dedicated his life to public service.[359]

Cornelius Aloysius O'Donnell was born in Bayonne, New Jersey, on Friday, August 8, 1902, to Neil and Sara O'Donnell, who were immigrants from Ireland. The O'Donnells had six children: Daniel, Mary, William, Cornelius, Rose and Flavin. Neil and Sara O'Donnell resided at 335 Kennedy Boulevard in Bayonne, a home that Neil built with his own hands. It was a two-family residence with seven rooms.[360]

Cornelius Aloysius O'Donnell
#367.

The O'Donnells were Irish Catholic and gave their children a parochial education. Neil O'Donnell was illiterate and wanted his children to have the best education. Cornelius attended St. Mary's Parochial School. Later in life, Neil's daughter Rose taught her father how to read. Afterward, the elder O'Donnell could be seen reading the morning newspaper at the kitchen table.[361]

After school, Cornelius worked various jobs until he became a carpenter for the City of Bayonne. O'Donnell's endeavors from his days as a carpenter up until his application to the state police aren't known. (All the O'Donnell children have passed away. The only family members remaining are his nephews.)[362] History records O'Donnell becoming a trooper on Monday, March 15, 1928, as a member of the sixteenth class. The twenty-five-year-old began his state police sojourn working in Troop B.[363]

In November 1931, O'Donnell was promoted to corporal. By July 1934, O'Donnell was second in charge at the Pompton Lakes Station. Sergeant John Doyle #287 was the station commander, and the camaraderie O'Donnell and Doyle had is described by *Paterson Evening News* editor Abe Green: "The team of O'Donnell and Sergeant John Doyle, has been helpful and efficient."[364]

In July 1934, despite the citizen outcry, O'Donnell was transferred to the Netcong Station. Four years later, he was promoted to sergeant.[365]

By 1938, O'Donnell's brother, William, was living downstairs at his parents' house. The O'Donnells were close, and oftentimes the family gathered for laughter and good times. Cornelius O'Donnell, or "Uncle Dick," as his nephews fondly called him, would crack everyone up with his various imitations. It became common to see Uncle Dick performing his Adolph Hitler imitation. To this day, these gatherings and Uncle Dick's playful persona hold a special place in his relatives' hearts. He was a loving uncle, and his love was returned.[366]

Conversely, a man named Ernest Rittenhouse was the polar opposite of Cornelius O'Donnell. Rittenhouse was cold, abusive and mentally unstable. He lived in Orange, New Jersey, with his wife and three children and struggled with his mental health throughout his life. He was in and out of mental hospitals, and on one occasion he managed to escape. O'Donnell was one of the troopers who captured Rittenhouse. Rittenhouse's parents lived in a town that was patrolled by troopers out of the Washington Station.[367]

On Saturday, July 14, 1945, Rittenhouse went into a rage and attacked his wife with an axe. Rittenhouse's children discovered their mother clinging to life on the floor and called the police. When authorities arrived at the home at 535 Liberty Street, they were met with a horrific scene. There was nothing a responder could do to save the woman. An all-points bulletin was put out on Rittenhouse, and the Orange Police Department notified the state police at the Washington Barracks, believing that Rittenhouse would once again flee to his parents' home in Brainards.[368]

The following morning, O'Donnell was briefed on the murder. He grabbed Trooper Frank Perry #565 and headed out to the Rittenhouse home in Brainards. O'Donnell had encountered Rittenhouse before, and presumably he believed he could bring him in again.[369]

By 1945, the forty-two-year-old O'Donnell was the station commander at Washington, and his belief in forming relationships with the community is highlighted by his involvement in the Rittenhouse case. He would often leave the comforts of his desk and get out to interact with the community he served.[370]

O'Donnell and Perry arrived at the Rittenhouse home and were met by an uncooperative father. O'Donnell told the man that "if he was harboring his son, he would be prosecuted to the full extent of the law." The man admitted that his son had spent the night, sleeping on spread-out papers in the basement. In the morning, he was given breakfast and left. The troopers

"Uncle Dick."

were two hours behind Rittenhouse and were told the killer had fled in a "southeasterly direction."[371]

The two troopers plotted the direction they believed Rittenhouse had taken and found themselves at the railroad trestle crossing at Martin's Creek. Martin's Creek is actually a portion of the Delaware River that separates New Jersey and Pennsylvania. The trestle crosses that divide. Believing that Rittenhouse had crossed the trestle and escaped into Pennsylvania, the two walked across the bridge, entering into Pennsylvania. An off-duty soldier told the troopers that he had seen a disheveled man enter a shed on the property of the Alpha Portland Cement Company. With guns drawn, O'Donnell and Perry found Rittenhouse in a run-down shed. He gave up without resistance.[372]

It is believed that the troopers tried to call Pennsylvania authorities, but the phone lines were out due to an overnight storm. They decided to go back to their car and radio in that they had apprehended the fugitive. While walking on the trestle, Rittenhouse pushed off the hold they had on him, and a struggle ensued. Rittenhouse got the better of the two and grabbed O'Donnell's gun. A shot rang out, and then another echoed over Martin's Creek. When it was all over, O'Donnell lay dead and Perry had been shot in the chest. The crazed man plunged into Martin's Creek, with Perry shooting three rounds as Rittenhouse swam away. All three shots struck their target, hitting Rittenhouse in the left cheek, his neck and under his chin. However, all were superficial wounds.[373]

Twelve hours after O'Donnell was gunned down, Rittenhouse was captured. The killer avoided the death penalty and was placed in a mental institution.[374]

On Thursday, July 19, a funeral Mass was held at St. Joseph's Church in Washington Township on Belvedere Avenue. O'Donnell was buried at the Gates of Heaven Cemetery in East Hanover, New Jersey, where hundreds of law enforcement personnel gathered to pay respects. As O'Donnell's casket was laid in his grave, a torrential downpour began. Family members say it was as if the heavens were crying at the loss of a great man.[375]

Cornelius Aloysius O'Donnell was survived by his wife, Alice Dee. The couple had no children. O'Donnell was forty-two years old.[376]

EXCESSIVE SPEED

Charles Kopf #905

Egg Harbor, New Jersey, is a community that dates back to 1693, when it was part of Gloucester County. Located in the Pine Barren area, Egg Harbor supposedly got its name from the Dutch explorer Cornelius Jacobsen Mey, who saw all the meadows covered with bird eggs and called this area *Eyren Haven*, which means Egg Harbor. By the 1920s, fewer than three thousand people called Egg Harbor home. On May 23, 1925, Egg Harbor resident Joseph Kopf increased the population by one with the birth of Charles Joseph Kopf.[377]

Kopf's father and his wife lived in Egg Harbor and owned a home at 206 Liverpool Avenue. Mr. and Mrs. Kopf were devout Catholics with a deep faith and a strong belief in religious education. Charles was sent to St. Nicholas Parochial School on Chicago Avenue through eighth grade. Afterward, he attended Egg Harbor High School. Nothing is known of Kopf's childhood.[378]

After school, Kopf worked for the New Jersey Tobacco Company in nearby Atlantic City. Atlantic City in the mid-1940s wasn't what it is today. Small, intimate hotels and casinos occupied the city, and up-and-coming entertainers like Dean Martin, Jerry Lewis and Frank Sinatra played to smoke-filled rooms with whiskey-drinking patrons. How long, and in what capacity, Charles Kopf served with the tobacco company cannot be determined.[379]

During the year 1947, Charles Kopf began going through the selection process for the upcoming thirty-fourth state police class. On December 16,

Charles Joseph Kopf #905.

Kopf graduated along with Trooper Walter Gawryla #902, who, like Kopf, died in the line of duty.[380]

Kopf was assigned to Troop C, and during his tenure he performed a mix of general police duties as well as highway patrol. Little of Kopf's career is known other than that he began his career on a cold December's day and ended it on a warm September day.[381]

By 1948, Charles Kopf was working out of the Columbus Barracks, where John Divers #127 had once worked. As a trooper, Kopf had a great deal of authority. Troopers have the authority to enforce all state laws and local ordinance and are empowered with the same authority as game wardens, who can enforce fish and game laws. The twenty-two-year-old handled this authority well and proved to be a good trooper.[382]

About this time, Kopf met Jane L. Betts, a resident of Absecon, New Jersey. The two were wed on Sunday, May 16, 1948. The young couple resided with Kopf's parents and were saving money in the hopes of one day having their own home. However, this was not to be.[383]

In the early morning hours of Monday, September 27, 1948, Kopf was on patrol in the vicinity of Hamilton Township. It was a nice day with a bright blue sky as he drove his 1947 black-and-white troop car, #C-207, down the road. As he did, the police radio sounded Kopf's car number, sending him to investigate a motor vehicle accident. Kopf headed north on the Crosswicks-Yardville Road in Hamilton (today the Yardville-Allentown Road). Meanwhile, a truck with a driver who had been drinking and was sleep deprived was speeding on State Highway 25 (today U.S. 130) in Kopf's direction. According to witnesses, the truck turned quickly into Kopf's lane, giving little time to react. The impact caused Kopf to be ejected, and he died as a result of his injuries.[384]

The funeral service was held on Thursday, September 30, at St. Nicholas's Church in Egg Harbor. Charles Kopf was buried in the Egg Harbor Cemetery on Moss Mill Road. Charles Joseph Kopf was twenty-three years old.[385]

A postscript to this story is that future New Jersey state trooper Ron Perozzi #2081 was taken in by Charles Kopf's parents, and he remembers that every night Kopf's mother would kneel down at an altar she had set up that included a picture of her son. Together, Kopf's parents and Ron Perozzi would "pray for his soul."[386]

STOP SIGN

Walter R. Gawryla #902

Walter Gawryla (pronounced Govarla) used to play in the streets of Garfield, New Jersey. Families had been raising children here dating back to 1000 BC, when the Leni-Lenape Indians homesteaded there because of its position on the banks of the Passaic River. Prior to the First World War, Gabriel and Mary emigrated from a small town near the Polish/Ukrainian border to the United States. Gawryla is of Ukrainian origin. Gabriel's vocation was that of a baker, while Mary stayed home. In 1916, their first child, a daughter named Jean, was born. Two years later, Frank followed, and on Wednesday, August 20, 1919, Walter Robert Gawryla was born.[387]

The Gawrylas lived during an interesting time in American history; the Industrial Revolution was in full effect, and Prohibition was the law of the land. The Industrial Revolution created mass production with the birth of the assembly line. As mass production increased, the American standard of living increased as well. Americans were buying the new products that came off those assembly lines. Products like dishwashers, refrigerators and sewing machines were becoming popular. The Industrial Revolution was responsible for increasing the ranks of the middle class. During this period, Gabriel and Mary bought a two-story home nestled close to the beautiful Passaic River in Wallington.[388]

Gabriel and Mary were devout Catholics and provided their children with a parochial education, sending Walter to Stanislaus Kustka Parochial School in town. After grammar school, he attended Lincoln High School #6.[389]

Walter Robert Gawryla #902.

Upon graduating, Gawryla found it difficult to get a job, as this was during the Great Depression. Nonetheless, he was ambitious and found a job as a machine mechanic. Then, on a beautiful Sunday morning in December, America was attacked at Pearl Harbor. This pivotal event caused droves of American men to enlist, and Gawryla was one of them. During his army service, Gawryla was a military motorcycle policeman in Europe.[390]

After his tour of duty, Gawryla applied to the state police for employment and was selected for academy training. On Thursday, December 18, 1947, with the wind blowing briskly, both Charles Kopf and Walter Gawryla exited their vehicles and reported to Troop C Headquarters for their first day as troopers.[391]

For the next two years, Gawryla performed his job with due diligence and adherence to the core values of the organization's credo of honor, duty and fidelity. Drawing from his military police background, Gawryla carried out his duties as a trooper on motorcycle.[392]

On Thursday, September 1, 1949, a warm day with a gentle breeze, Walter Gawryla reported to the Flemington Barracks in Troop B. For the next seven months, he could be seen patrolling the rural towns. During this period, Gawryla met a woman named Olga. The two wed on January 28, 1950. Sometime during this period, Walter's father, Gabriel, died. It isn't known if he had lived to see the marriage. Soon after the wedding, Olga became pregnant, and by summer their daughter was born.[393]

On Wednesday, April 19, 1950, a clear spring day with temperatures in the mid-seventies, history records Walter Gawryla on patrol with his brand-new Harley Davidson motorcycle #405. He was throttling north on State Highway 30 (present-day State Highway 31) in Raritan Township in Hunterdon County and was approaching the intersection that meets with Pennsylvania Avenue. Traveling on Pennsylvania Avenue was Ann Bonney Cole, a woman in her early twenties with little driving experience. Cole approached the intersection and failed to see the trooper on motorcycle pulling directly into his path. The impact was swift and deadly for Walter Gawryla.[394]

The news of Walter Gawryla's death was crippling. It was a new decade for the New Jersey State Police, one that would see the organization expand its numbers to nearly five hundred troopers. It also would be a decade that would witness one trooper death after another—eleven in all.[395]

It was raining and fog filled the air when Walter Robert Gawryla was laid to rest at St. Michael's Cemetery on Main Street in Lodi, New Jersey. He was thirty years old.[396]

FATE

Emil J. Bock #974

Many troopers were born in Bayonne, New Jersey; several of them died in the line of duty. Emil Joseph Bock was one of these fine troopers, born on October 25, 1926, to Stanley and Elizabeth Bock. Stanley and Elizabeth lived during a tumultuous time in American history. A week before Emil's birth, a group of bandits brandished a submachine gun and robbed a mail truck in the nearby city of Elizabeth, killing the driver.[397]

The name of Bock is believed to be of German/Polish descent, and records report several Bocks fighting in the Revolutionary War. Elizabeth Bock (née Bobal) was of German heritage. Four children were born to the Bocks: Emil, Edward, Thomas and Adele. The ages of the Bock children isn't clear, but it is believed that Emil was the eldest.[398]

While Emil was attending high school, his generation enjoyed listening to Bing Crosby and watching popular stars such as Cary Grant, Clark Gable, Humphrey Bogart and James Cagney grace the silver screen. When Bock graduated in 1944, the eighteen-year-old stood nearly six feet tall, weighed 180 pounds and spoke fluent Slovak. During this time, the United States was engaged in World War II, and Bock served in the navy for two years.[399]

Upon leaving the military, Bock attended college in Union, New Jersey, studying radio and electrical theory. His tenure at Union College lasted three years before he left to work as an electronics instructor.[400]

The 1950s witnessed a change in the American landscape, especially in and around the city of Bayonne. The events of the 1940s had brought about suburbia and the expansion of the middle class. New jobs were being created,

Emil Joseph Bock #974.

providing the American worker with more opportunities. Around this time, Emil Bock applied to be a Jersey trooper.[401] On a cold December day, Bock held out his hand and accepted his state police badge. Characteristic of the day, the twenty-three-year-old trooper was sent in the complete opposite direction of where he lived: south Jersey. Bock's first day as a state trooper was Tuesday, December 26, 1950.[402]

The most significant event in Bock's career took place over a month before his fateful accident. Leo J. Coakley covers this incident in his book *Jersey Troopers*. A former trooper, Coakley stated that Bock made an arrest and was transporting his prisoner back to the station when the prisoner attempted to escape. A struggle ensued in the troop car, and Bock lost control of his car and crashed into a tree. After the impact, the prisoner got out of the car and tried to grab Bock's gun. When the ordeal ended, the prisoner was dead. Bock understood as a trooper he might be faced with the prospect of taking a life, and even though it was traumatic, he moved on with performing his sworn duties.[403]

At this period, Bock was fully entangled in a romance with a woman from his neighborhood named Lucille Tworkoski. She soon became the twinkle in his brown eyes. Lucille lived at 21 West Thirtieth Street, which was a short distance from Bock's home at 11A West Thirtieth Street. Bock was still living with his parents, and the convenience of proximity allowed for frequent visits. Emil and Lucille began planning their wedding, and in accordance with state police policy, Bock requested permission from the superintendent of state police to marry. On Friday, April 20, 1951, Emil Bock sat down at the manual typewriter in the Berlin Station and typed: "The undersigned respectfully requests that permission be granted to marry Miss Lucille Tworkoski…If granted the ceremony will take place at Mount Carmel Church Bayonne N.J. on June 23 1951."[404]

Less than a month before his marriage, on May 26, 1951, Bock walked out of the station and felt a cool breeze on his face as he mounted his motorcycle. In the early hours of the day, he was on State Highway 41 in Berlin when he was met with an accident. As Bock was traveling south, a woman named Anna Slover, who was traveling north, made a U-turn through the median, directly in the path of Bock. This accident isn't much different than those of Vosbein, Arrowsmith or Perry; sadly, neither is the outcome. Bock met his demise as a result of an inattentive driver.[405] Bock was rushed to Cooper Hospital in Camden, where doctors worked audaciously on him. Despite the prayers of his loved ones, he passed away at the age of twenty-four.[406]

The funeral for the fallen trooper was held on Thursday, May 31, at St. Joseph's Roman Catholic Church on Twenty-fifth Street in Bayonne. He was laid to rest at the Holy Cross Cemetery in North Arlington, New Jersey.[407]

KICKSTAND

Stanley A. Conn Jr. #947

New Jersey state trooper Stanley Conn was only twenty-five years old when he died, struck down in the prime of life. He had it all: a good job, a wife and two small children, one of whom was only a few months old. His story begins in a small hamlet and ends on a lonely roadway.[408]

Stanley Arlington Conn Jr. was born on August 6, 1926. Conn Sr. was of Scottish descent, and his wife, Charlotte, was Irish. Conn Sr. was from Netcong, New Jersey, in rural Morris County, and his wife was from nearby Stanhope. When they wed, the couple moved to 79 Allen Street in Netcong. It was a two-story, three-bedroom house that was brown with white shingles. Stanley Conn was a railroad worker for the Delaware, Lackawanna and Western (DL&W) Railroad. The railroad supported the vast majority of residents living in and around the Morris County area. Stanley and Charlotte had four children: Gertrude, Edith, James and Stanley. The elder Conn worked for the railroad until he was diagnosed with cancer at the age of thirty-nine. He struggled with the illness, spending a year in the hospital, and died at the age of forty. His son Stanley was only six years old.[409]

Charlotte was a strong Irish woman who raised four children on her own. In September 1931, Stanley began school at the Netcong Grammar School and completed his education there in June 1939. The Conn brothers spent a lot of time together; in the winter, the lake in town would freeze, and they played ice hockey. In the summer and fall, the brothers played football and went camping. "We had a lot of fun," said James Conn. Stanley Conn graduated high school at age sixteen.[410]

Stanley Arlington Conn Jr. #947.

Conn began working immediately as a clerk with the DL&W Railroad, which paid him $1,800 a year. In February 1944, he left the railroad because of a lack of work. A month later, Conn found a job working at the Picatinny Arsenal in northwest Morris County. On Monday, August 14, 1944, Conn enlisted in the United States Naval Reserve. He was shipped overseas and, while there, met up with his brother James. The visit came as a surprise, as Stanley didn't know that James was on the same base. The brothers spent quality time together before resuming their military duties. During his tenure, Conn rose to the rank of seaman first class, and on Tuesday, June 13, 1944, he left the service with an honorable discharge.[411]

Conn took several technical courses on engine repair, receiving instruction on diesel and gas engine maintenance and repair from the Hemphill Diesel School in New York. After nine months, he received a certification for engine repair. Sometime during this period, he met a woman who captured his heart. Her name was Frances, and she was a year younger than Conn and lived at 340 Van Nostrand Avenue in Jersey City. On Saturday, September 13, 1947, Stanley and Frances were wed. Conn's employment prior to his wedding and up until the fall of 1948 isn't known. After celebrating their first anniversary, he was again working for the railroad as a plumber's helper with a yearly salary of $3,000 However, in March 1949, he left to work as a mechanic helper for Brewer and Le Blanc Motors. It is interesting to note that Conn took this position even though it paid almost half of what the railroad had paid.[412]

Two months after his twenty-third birthday, Conn was working at the Davey Company in Jersey City as a laborer manufacturing binder boards. This job was the highest paying he had thus far, paying him $3,400 a year. This was noteworthy, considering the average salary in the country was about $1,300. During this time, Stanley and Frances were living at 285 Stegman Parkway in Jersey City. And even though Conn was making an impressive salary, he filled out a state police application.[413]

The year 1950 was a busy one for the Conns. Stanley and Frances were expecting their first child, and Conn began training to become a trooper. On Thursday, February 2, 1950, Stanley A. Conn III was born, and five months later, on Friday, July 28, Conn became a Jersey trooper. His service with the "outfit" would be brief. Two of the stations he worked at were Berkeley Heights and Pompton Lakes. In April 1951, a second child was born to the couple, a daughter named Kathleen.[414]

Conn is in the second row, second from left.

On Monday, August 6, 1951, Stanley celebrated his twenty-fifth birthday. He was thankful for all he and Frances had. Two weeks later, history records Conn working out of the Pompton Lakes Station on Monday, August 27, 1951.[415]

Trooper Conn kick-started his motorcycle and throttled north on Hamburg Turnpike, pulling out of the station parking lot. His early morning activities are not known other than that he had breakfast at the Pompton Diner on Wanaque Avenue at 9:00 a.m. Afterward, Conn headed south on Wanaque Avenue toward the monument that divides Hamburg Turnpike and Wanaque Avenue. Upon approaching that divide, the trooper leaned his bike to the right in order to head west on Hamburg Turnpike. As he did so, his kickstand came loose and dug into the pavement. This caused the motorcycle to go out of control, and Conn was thrown head first into an oncoming car. A local doctor arrived within minutes to aid the fallen trooper, but there was nothing he could do to save the man.[416]

Stanley Arlington Conn Jr.'s funeral was held on Friday, August 31, with the Mass taking place at Our Lady of Sorrows Roman Catholic Church in Jersey City. Stanley Conn was laid to rest at the Holy Cross Cemetery in North Arlington, New Jersey.[417]

STRANGE

Joseph D. Wirth #943

On June 8, 1926, Joseph Daniel Wirth Jr. was born to Joseph and Hannah Wirth. Joseph's father came from modest beginnings, as his father was a German immigrant baker from Hoboken, New Jersey. Hannah's mother, Helen Browley, was born of Irish immigrants who migrated to Bayonne. Helen's mother, Margerete (née Connor), was born in Cork, Ireland. Margarete married James Hurley, a second-generation Irishman from Bayonne, and that's where Hannah was born. It is presumed that Joseph Wirth Sr. lived in Bayonne and that is how the two met. The couple was wed in a ceremony at St. Andrew's Church in the city.[418]

Joseph and Hannah moved to 69 Garretson Avenue, which was a two-story, three-bedroom home a few blocks away from the Newark Bay and the Kill van Kull River. Joseph and Hannah had five children: Joseph, Margarete, James, John and Helen. The Wirths were Catholic and sent their children to St. Andrew's Parish School.[419] After grammar school, Joseph Wirth Jr. attended Henry Harris Junior High School and then went on to Bayonne Technical and Vocational High School.[420]

By seventeen years old, Wirth stood six feet, three inches tall and weighed 220 pounds. He had grown to become a handsome man with brown hair, a light complexion and blue eyes. At this age, he dropped out of school and enlisted in the United States Navy. On Wednesday, January 19, 1944, the navy sent him to the University of Chicago to study naval communications. Afterward, he was assigned to the USS *Mississippi*, a warship that was commissioned in December 1917. The *Mississippi* saw action during both

Joseph Daniel Wirth #943.

world wars and, during World War II, survived two Kamikaze attacks. Wirth served his entire tenure overseas.[421]

After his discharge, Wirth found it difficult to find a job and, along with several of his military buddies, joined the "52 Club," an organization where members were helped financially until they found employment. Wirth's uncle, Raymond Wirth #451, was a Jersey trooper, and his stories compelled Joseph to apply.[422]

On Monday, August 29, 1949, members of the thirty-sixth state police class gathered under clear skies and warm weather to graduate. Wirth took part in a motorcycle demonstration that was put on for family and friends. After the presentation, members were called up to receive their triangular state police badges.[423]

Wirth's tenure with the New Jersey State Police was short-lived, with little documented of his tenure. Wirth's sister Peggy remembers that her brother started out as a motorcycle trooper and had a serious accident early on that left him with a broken leg. Interestingly, an off-duty incident brings Joseph Wirth's name to the forefront of state police history. Wirth is listed as dying in the line of duty; however, the incident that claimed his life took place while he was off duty and celebrating the Thanksgiving holiday with a high school friend.[424]

It was November 25, 1951, and Wirth was out with his friend John Foley in New York City. While returning home, with Wirth driving Foley's 1949 Red Mercury convertible, the two entered the city of Bayonne. As they were traveling south on Kennedy Boulevard, Wirth turned left to enter Thirty-fifth Avenue. Apparently, he did not see an oncoming vehicle and drove directly in front of the car. The impact killed Wirth instantly, and Foley died six days later. The occupants of the other vehicle all received minor injuries.[425]

On Tuesday, August 5, 1952, the superintendent's office prepared a memorandum to the state attorney general reporting: "Trooper Joseph D. Wirth was killed in an automobile accident in Bayonne, New Jersey on 25 November 1951…He was off duty at the time, riding in the automobile of a friend."[426]

Joseph Wirth was buried on Wednesday, November 28, 1951, at the Holy Cross Cemetery in North Arlington, New Jersey. He was twenty-five years old.[427]

OVERTURN

Joseph C. Walter #685

Joseph and Anna Walter lived on Ann Street in Newark, New Jersey, and were German immigrants. Anna's parents were Meinrod and Carolyn Schuler. The names of Joseph's parents aren't known. On May 25, 1912, Anna gave birth to Joseph C. Walter Jr. at their home on Ann Street. Later, the couple moved to a larger home at 124 Locust Street in Roselle Park, New Jersey. Walter was a postal worker in the nearby city of Irvington, and Anna was a homemaker. Anna made sure that her husband's food was on the table every day when he returned home. They had a pleasant home atmosphere that was rooted in Catholicism. When Joseph was of age, he attended St. Joseph's Parochial School in Roselle Park. In 1919, a second child, Frank, was born to the couple.[428]

In 1926, Walter graduated to St. Benedict's Preparatory School in Newark. There, Walter had a wonderful time. He had an innate athletic ability and excelled in the school's sports programs. He played football during the fall and baseball in the spring. One day while Walter was practicing baseball, a member of the track team overthrew a javelin, landing it next to Walter. When asked to throw it back, Walter set the "unofficial" record for javelin throwing. During his high school years, Joseph Walter became the football captain and in 1930 was awarded All-State End of the Year. As a baseball player, he was a catcher. By the time of his graduation, Walter had grown to be five feet, eight inches. He had brown hair, blue eyes and a stocky frame with "thunderous legs." In his high school yearbook, one classmate wrote that Walter was "a Prince of a fellow."[429]

Joseph C. Walter Jr. #685.

After school, Walter entered a world that was in an economic crisis. The Great Depression was in full effect, with almost one in four people unemployed. Walter's drive for sports led to an unsuccessful tryout with the New York Giants football team at the polo grounds. This tryout led to another with the Newark Bears football team, which was a minor league team that drafted him. After his football career ended, Walter secured a job working for the Fupot Company in Grasselli, New Jersey, and was eventually promoted to foreman. By all indications, Walter maintained this position until he became a Jersey trooper.[430]

On November 14, 1938, the New Jersey State Police issued Special Order #666, announcing the graduation of the twenty-seventh state police class. The number, often associated with the mark of the devil, cast a dark shadow over the members of this class, several of whom died in the line of duty.[431]

Upon receiving his triangular badge, Walter was assigned to Troop B. He was a hard worker and learned his job well, developing sharp investigative skills. Before long, Walter was made an investigator, the equivalent of a detective. In the early years of his career, Walter met a woman and was engaged to marry her when another caught his eye.[432]

Miriam O'Rourke was born on June 11, 1915, and was an attractive woman who stood five feet, four inches tall, with a slender figure. She was walking her dog in Roselle Park when she bumped into Joseph Walter. Walter felt an instant attraction, as did Miriam. This created an obstacle for Miriam, as the impressive trooper was about to be married. According to the Walter sisters, their Aunt Eileen used to tell the story of how Miriam swept Walter off his feet. She used to walk the dog in hopes of seeing him. Her efforts paid off. The couple wed on Saturday, March 15, 1941.[433]

Walter took his city girl and moved her to a farmhouse in Sussex County on County Route 565. The farm sat north of what is now known as Ross's Corner, in a section called Pellet Town. The farm consisted of five acres of spacious open land with horses and farm animals. For Miriam, it proved to be a difficult transition. Route 565 cuts between farms on each side, with the closest store miles away. Three years after their wedding, they celebrated the birth of their first child on March 4, 1943—a girl named Eileen. Two years later, Patricia was born on August 31, 1945. As his family was expanding, Walter had been working hard as an investigator, first out of the Sussex Barracks and then out of the Newton Barracks. Fortunately, both assignments were close to the Walter farm. From time to time, he found time to stop home during work to have lunch or just see his wife and children. On May 20, 1950, the Walters' last child, Karen, was born.[434]

In January 1951, the title of investigator was abolished by the state police, and Walter resumed normal trooper duties. While home, Walter could be seen riding horses with his wife and children. Often, the family would head into Sussex Borough for dinner. The two would have fun making their daughter Patty dance for pizza. Working out of the Sussex Area—where troopers patrol the local towns—Walter became friendly with many business owners. He was a gregarious person, warm and sincere, who was very respected. He was a religious man, too, with a devout faith in God. He believed in good over evil and dedicated his life to ensure that the citizens he served were defended against unlawful behavior. As a constant reminder of his faith, he always wore a medal of St. Christopher. Often Walter could be seen holding and rubbing the medal. On Sundays, the Walters attended church at St. Monicors in Sussex County, where Walter's old friend Father Christian Haag was the pastor.[435]

Walter's daughters were always happy to see "Daddy," especially when he came home on his big motorcycle. Walter gave his children rides and used to zigzag down the road with his daughters laughing and having a blast. Joseph Walter's daughters have fond memories of their father. And even though they didn't have him in their lives for long, they are thankful for the times they shared. "I remember," says Eileen, "my dad taking me to the jail in Newton and showing us what it was like to be in jail." There are many memories like this for the Walter children.[436]

On August 12, 1952, Walter was scheduled off and planned on having fun on the farm with his wife and children. However, his plans were disrupted when Trooper F. Skok #802 called out because his wife went into labor. Walter volunteered to work in his place.[437]

It was a miserable day with heavy rain. Walter had been working a bizarre case in which a woman shot her husband, mistaking him for a groundhog.

Trooper Skok is third from left, and Walter is fourth from left.

It kept Walter engrossed. During the day, he was out with Trooper Anthony Ciaramella #1086, and the two were following up leads. About 2:20 p.m., they were driving north on State Highway 23 with Ciaramella behind the wheel of a state police jeep. For reasons not known, Ciaramella lost control and ran up an embankment, overturning the vehicle. The accident occurred in front of a place called the Castle Inn. A more accurate marking of this site is mile post 36.5. The Castle Inn has been out of business for years and is now an electronics store. After overturning, the jeep slid into the opposite lane of travel and was struck by an oncoming car.[438]

Walter injured his back and hip and had numerous abrasions and contusions and a fracture of his vertebrae. The injuries were classified as non–life threatening. A long hospital stay was expected, with a full recovery. During Walter's stay, Miriam and the children visited him daily. Eileen and Patty remember that the hospital staff would not allow their sister Karen, who was just a baby, in to see their father. The sisters would pass Karen through the window into the room when no one was looking. Holding his little baby made Walter's stay a little brighter.[439]

Then, on September 7, Walter had a sudden decline in his health, and it was determined that he had a blood clot. Cardiologists discussed a course of action to deal with the blood clot, but before anything could be done, he passed away. According to the doctors, "His demise was sudden and unexpected." The cause of death was listed as "Pulmonary Embolism"—in essence, the clot had entered his lungs and killed him.[440]

The funeral for Joseph C. Walter Jr. was held on September 10, 1952, at 9:30 a.m. at St. Joseph's Church. Walter's friend Father Christian Haag performed the service. Joseph Walter was forty years old.[441]

NEW JERSEY TURNPIKE

Frank A. Trainor #682

Frank Trainor was born on Monday, July 14, 1913, in Philadelphia, Pennsylvania, and was raised in Pleasantville, New Jersey, in Atlantic County in the south Jersey region. Trainor received his sole education through the Pleasantville school system.[442]

How do we pay tribute to a man when little is documented of his existence? What is known is that he lived at 142 River Road in May's Landing, New Jersey. Let us presume a few things, such as that his first name was actually Francis. His middle name isn't known, but his surname is derived from the Gaelic word Treunmhor, or Treun, both of which mean "very brave." The family of Trainors comes from Dublin City and the districts between Monaghan, Armagh and Dungannon in Ireland.[443]

That being said, let us begin with what is known. Frank A. Trainor began training for the state police in mid-1938. He graduated on Monday, August 15, as a member of the twenty-seventh class. Trainor spent the bulk of his career in south Jersey and was eventually transferred to the New Jersey Turnpike. By August 1953, Trainor had nearly fifteen years on the job and was a sergeant. Interestingly, Sergeant Trainor would become the third state police sergeant killed in the line of duty out of only four in the whole history of the organization. Moreover, he was the first of many troopers who had his last patrol on the New Jersey Turnpike.[444]

On Monday, August 3, 1953, Sergeant Trainor was working on the New Jersey Turnpike in the early morning hours. At about 6:08 a.m., he spotted a car committing a violation and pulled the vehicle over. The violator pulled

Frank A Trainor #682.

to the shoulder at mile post 38 (the stop occurred 376 feet north of the mile marker). The stop was on the southbound portion of the highway. At the time, the road consisted of four lanes—two north and two south—with a grass median separating them.[445]

The documentation on this accident is incomplete. According to witnesses, Trainor approached the violator and asked the driver for his paperwork. Upon taking the documents, he began walking back to his troop car, and just as he neared the rear of the stopped car, a truck struck him, catapulting Trainor over the car and facedown on the shoulder. The state police sergeant was killed instantly.[446]

The driver of the truck, Gerald W. Lavigne of 193 Green Street in Manchester, New Hampshire, was charged with reckless driving and death by auto. Records are incomplete as to the outcome of these charges. Frank A. Trainor was only forty years old.[447]

ROBBERY, MURDER AND THE TAKING OF A HOSTAGE ON ROUTE 66

John Anderson #1191

John Anderson was born in Dover, New Jersey, on March 19, 1919, to Charles and Anna, who were poor Russian immigrants who changed their name from Andronshik to Anderson. Charles found gainful employment working as a coal miner in the mountains of Carbondale, Pennsylvania, where the first underground mine was built. Upon settling there, the Andersons began growing their family with the birth of their daughter Mary in 1914. Soon, John, Helen and Charles followed.[448]

The patriarch's paycheck kept food on the table but left little for anything else. The couple couldn't afford a house and moved from apartment to apartment. Then suddenly, one night a fire broke out in their home, and they barely escaped out the upstairs window. It was a traumatic incident, never forgotten. Sadly, the building was destroyed, leaving them homeless.[449]

Fortunately, Charles and Anna found another apartment on Gordon Avenue in town. It is here that the Anderson children were raised to adulthood. They were all educated at the Carbondale schools, with John becoming a popular athlete, playing football for three years at Benjamin Franklin High. During a game, Anderson broke his leg, which ended his participation in the sport.[450]

At the age of eighteen, Anderson stood six feet tall, had a muscular build and had light brown hair with hazel eyes. With the onset of World War II, Anderson entered the United States Army and served overseas. During his tour, he rose to the rank of master sergeant and left the service with an honorable discharge.[451]

John Anderson #1191.

After the service, Anderson taught at Rutgers University for its ROTC program, and during this period he met a woman named Jean (last name unknown).[452]

On Sunday, April 12, 1953, John Anderson graduated from the forty-third state police class and was assigned to Troop A. There, he worked for just about a year before being transferred to the Garden State Parkway. The order came on July 29, 1954, that he would be assigned to the Holmdel Station. After a year's service on the highway, in April 1955, the state police merged the parkway with the turnpike, forming Troop D. Unfortunately, Anderson's tenure in the new troop would be short-lived, as his encounter with a man named Sammy Alvarez was only months away.[453]

Route 66 is a well-known highway, immortalized in movies, television, literature and song. The highway stretches from Chicago to Los Angeles and was once called the "Mother Road," and its popularity has been illustrated time and again. "Get your kicks on Route 66" is a phrase from a popular song. The United States worked for years to build interstate highways, known as the Eisenhower Interstate Highway System. Today, these "superhighways" take people across the country in little time compared to the days when highways like Route 66 linked rural roads to urban communities. Route 66 was one of the first of these highways and is now part of American folklore. In New Jersey, there is also a highway called Route 66. The stories of this Route 66 are few, but one such story involves the murder of a New Jersey state trooper and a horrifying hostage situation. It was an incident that sent chills down the backs of local residents whose homes were near Route 66.[454]

This story begins with Mrs. Bernice Ashton, a married woman from Neptune, New Jersey, who was out one night trying to forget her woes. Ashton had separated from her husband, and on this particular evening, a young man caught her eye. It was mid-September 1955, a little over a year after the Supreme Court made its famous decision overturning the "separate but equal" doctrine in the case of *Brown v. Board of Education*. It took a long time before public establishments began to follow the ruling's footsteps. On this particular night, Ashton was out at an all-black establishment called the Chitterling Paradise when an attractive, mysterious man named Sammy Alvarez turned the heartache she felt into folly. Alvarez was a shady character with a thirst for booze. He turned on the charm and took the young woman's number, and soon the two became an item.[455]

This relationship moves us forward to a Tuesday evening in November, the date—November 1, 1955—when Alvarez stopped at Ashton's Neptune home with a friend. Ashton thought this strange, but Alvarez had robbery on his mind, not dating. He was planning a robbery of a local gas station. After leaving Ashton's place, Alvarez and Howard picked up another shady character named William Singletery, and the three headed to Straub's Gas Station on Route 35 in Keyport, New Jersey.[456] The men walked inside the place and, under guise of using the phone, gained access to the back room, where Alvarez subdued the worker. As the three left the station, a local resident spotted them leaving quickly and advised the authorities that they had departed in a 1955 Pontiac.[457]

John Anderson was working the Holmdel Station's book, or station log, when he heard the "be on the lookout" broadcast. Anderson wrote the information down and gave the call out to the troopers in the area: "Man believed to be armed," Anderson advised. "Use caution." A few minutes later, Anderson himself went out on patrol.[458]

It was a pleasant night with mild temperatures and a full moon, and as Anderson's shift progressed, traffic lightened. Three hours after that radio broadcast, Anderson observed a car parked in the center median at mile post 112.5 on the southbound side of the parkway. What happened next is speculation. A haunting radio transmission by John Anderson sent shivers down the backs of those hearing his voice cry out, "Help!" Silence filled the radio in the hopes that there would be a second transmission. Seconds felt like minutes before it came: "Help, Holmdel, help! I am at 112 on the medial strip."[459]

Troopers Anthony Scalzone #1270 and Henry Kalinowski #1258 rushed to the trooper's aid. When the two rolled up, they found Anderson slumped over his front seat with microphone in hand. Still conscious, Anderson performed what would be his last police function. He gave a partial plate number and lapsed into unconsciousness.[460]

Investigators speculate that Alvarez—for reasons never determined—had pulled his vehicle to the shoulder and was in the woods when Anderson pulled up. It is believed that Alvarez jumped Anderson and overpowered him, taking his gun. Three shots were fired, and the low-level criminal who had caught the eye of Bernice Ashton committed the most egregious criminal act: murder![461]

Looking "cool." *Courtesy of Helen Hartwiger.*

Within minutes, the biggest manhunt in the history of the Jersey Shore was underway. State Trooper Edward Wilke #1423 spotted Alvarez's vehicle on Highway 35 near the Asbury Traffic Circle and pursued the car. The chase ended on a dead-end street with Alvarez running into the woods as Wilke fired a shot at him. Moments later, five hundred lawmen surrounded the town of Neptune, along with firefighters and armed citizens. Able to elude the posse, Sammy Alvarez crawled out of the woods and into the Fernwood Motel on Route 66.[462]

Edward and Victoria Whritenour were owners of the motel and were relaxing in their living room when a knock came at the door. Whritenour was met by Alvarez. "He pulled out his pistol…I wanted to cooperate 100 percent," Whritenour recalled. "He was looking for an excuse to shoot." Alvarez forced Victoria to bind and gag her husband, and Alvarez shoved the proprietor into the bedroom closet.[463]

At first, Alvarez was nervous and kept looking out the window, but after a half hour or so, his deviant thirst beckoned and he began to fondle Victoria Whritenour. When she passed out, Alvarez picked her up and began carrying her to the bedroom so he could complete his dirty deed. However, he heard a loud noise from the closet and went to check. What Sammy Alvarez didn't know is that Whritenour had freed himself and grabbed a gun he had in his closet. As Alvarez entered the hall leading to the bedroom, Edward Whritenour peered out of the bedroom and fired one fatal shot into Alvarez's head.[464]

Just as the knock on Whritenour's door changed his life forever, so did the knock that came on Helen Hartwiger's door that same night. Anderson's sister remembers that when a trooper arrived to tell her the terrible news, she was listening to the song "Autumn Leaves." She has never forgotten that song.

Since you went away the days grow long
And soon I'll hear old winter's song
But I miss you most of all my darling
When autumn leaves start to fall.[465]

"FIGHT IN PROGRESS"

George Richard Dancy #1481

George Richard Dancy Jr. was born on March 9, 1933, in Schenectady, New York, to George and Catherine Dancy. The Dancys moved to Schenectady in the hopes of starting a family, but as time went on, the two drifted apart, leaving George as their only child. After their divorce, George ended up living with his father, who remarried and had three other children. For Dancy's mother, George was her only child.[466]

George initially attended high school in Scotia, New York, where his mother was living, but when his father moved to Caldwell, New Jersey, George moved to the Garden State with him. Caldwell is in Essex County and is known as the birthplace of Grover Cleveland, the United States' twenty-second and twenty-fourth President. Interestingly, Cleveland is the only president to serve two nonconsecutive terms. Dancy attended Grover Cleveland High School, where he met his high school sweetheart and future wife, Barbara.[467]

While at Grover Cleveland, Dancy played basketball, baseball and football. As an athlete, he always kept himself in good shape. And although he was busy with sports, Dancy always kept a close relationship with his siblings. He was an excellent role model, and his younger brother, David, was in awe of him. According to David, George was the perfect older brother.[468]

In his senior year of high school, 1951, George met a junior named Barbara Ann. Barbara fondly remembers their high school days. "We were introduced by a mutual friend," said Barbara. "We liked each other right away." It wasn't long before they were a couple. Barbara says that they

George Richard Dancy Jr.
#1481.

used to attend many dances, as George liked to dance: "he was quite good at it."[469]

During the summers, George worked down the shore as a lifeguard. However, one year George had yet to go down the shore while Barbara was on vacation on the Jersey beach with her family. This created a problem for George, having to remain in Caldwell while Barbara was on vacation. One day, while sunbathing, Barbara noticed a low-flying plane cruising the shoreline. As the plane grew closer, she noticed that a man was hanging out the door waving. Upon closer examination, she realized that it was George trying to get her attention. He had talked a friend who owned a plane into flying down there so he could see his sweetheart.[470]

After school, Dancy worked several odd jobs, one of which was with his dad, who owned a funeral parlor. George Sr. hired his son to work as a professional pallbearer, earning the man a hefty sum of twenty dollars for each funeral. As George matured, he developed an interest in furthering his education by attending college. By this point in his life, he was in love with Barbara, and the two began planning their life together. George applied to the University of Connecticut and attended there for only two semesters. His separation anxiety kept him from being able to focus on his studies. He returned home and asked Barbara to marry him. There was no hesitation on her part, and the two were wed on Sunday, October 5, 1952.[471]

Shortly after their wedding, George obtained a position with the United States Post Office in Essex Fells, a small community just outside of Caldwell. Soon, the couple enjoyed the birth of their first child, Cathy. The love for family that Dancy had showed as an older brother only increased as a father. George Dancy spent as much time with Cathy as he could. He was a doting father and a loving husband.[472]

Even though he had a job and a family, Dancy kept very involved in his community, counseling children in the neighborhood. The venue Dancy chose was the local Boy Scouts. Whether as a son, brother, husband, father or trooper, George Richard Dancy Jr. was an exceptional man. One only has to speak with his brother David to realize this. "George is my older brother," says David. "The quarterback, the point guard, the center fielder, the State Trooper, my hero."[473]

When George and Barbara were able to purchase their own home, they made sure it was close to his family. They resided at 10 Park Terrace in Caldwell. Always energetic, outgoing and motivated, George tried again to go to college. He began attending Rutgers University in Newark at night. His pursuit for higher education is remarkable considering at the time less than 10 percent of people in the country had a college degree. The strains of married life, raising a child, work and night school took their toll, and Dancy put his educational aspirations on hold. There would be time in the future, he thought.[474]

One day, while reading a newspaper, Dancy saw an ad for an upcoming New Jersey State Police examination. He was curious and pondered this prospect, discussing it with his wife. George "looked into it a little bit and said I think I might be able to do this," remembers Barbara. With Barbara's blessing, he took the test. She remembers that afterward, he was anxious to learn the results. "He paced the floor…until he got a letter saying he had passed the written exam," says Barbara.[475]

On August 28, 1955, George entered training for the fiftieth state police class and, according to Barbara, went through "sixteen weeks of hell." At the academy, Dancy looked forward to mail call and reading Barbara's letters. The academy was tremendously difficult, and Barbara noticed the strain it put on George. "I wrote him a letter," said Barbara, "telling him to hang in there." There were only a few weeks left, and George needed a little boost. The encouraging words of Barbara did the trick.[476]

On Friday, December 16, 1955, family and friends gathered for the graduation of the latest state police class. Four days later, Trooper Dancy

George and Cathy. *Courtesy of Barbara Hubscher.*

reported to work at 9:00 a.m. and was told that his assignment was the Riverton Barracks in Troop C. Barbara says that George loved the state police. He "really enjoyed the time he had with the state police...I can remember that the state police gave him a certain amount of respect. People called him sir, he was a kid, he was only twenty-three years old himself." Above all, George was a loving husband, father and brother. Not long after graduating, Barbara told George that she was expecting another child. He was ecstatic. The couple were enjoying their life together.[477]

With much anticipation, George and Barbara celebrated the New Year. The year 1956 turned out to be a year that changed pop culture and the American musical scene, due to a southerner from Memphis named Elvis Presley stepping into a recording studio. Sadly, the events of 1956 would not be so kind to the Dancy family and the New Jersey State Police as it was to Elvis.[478]

State troopers experience great dangers, many of which are taken for granted. The job is a dangerous one. Moreover, the dangers are not always the obvious ones. Many of the day-to-day functions that troopers perform can be perilous.[479]

It was a Monday night, May 28, 1956, to be exact, when Dancy's radio dispatched him to a fight in progress. He was working out of the Riverton Station at about 9:25 p.m. when the call came in. The fight was at a place called Martin's Inn in Springville, a small borough that is part of the larger Mount Laurel Township. Dancy was on Hartford Road in response to the call when he approached the intersection of Route 38. As he entered the intersection, an inattentive driver crossed directly into his path. The impact sent the troop car out of control and into a telephone pole, around which the car wrapped. Rescuers spent twenty minutes extricating the lifeless trooper from the wreck. Barbara remembers that night all too well:

> *When the two troopers came to my door, I didn't have a clue. I thought he was going to be in a hospital with a broken leg. Cathy was sleeping and one of the troopers went in and bundled her up and* [took] *her up a mile or two...to my mother-in-law's, while we made the trip to Bordentown. I wanted my father to go. I guess maybe I did know inside that something wasn't right.*[480]

According to Barbara, George had gone into a job he loved, and "that's the way he went out." David Dancy remembers the last time he saw his big brother:

I was at track practice at Caldwell High and he [Dancy] and a friend drove down in his old green 1949 Ford to see how I was doing. He watched from the hill for a while, then waved and said you are doing great Dave and drove off. The next thing I remember is it's 5:00 a.m. and I hear George's mother-in-law and our mother talking. I can't hear all the words...and got up the courage to walk down the hall to ask Mom what was going on...I learned that my hero would now be only a memory.[481]

George Dancy's second daughter, Chris, was born four months after his death. Barbara remarried a man named William Hubscher, and they had a daughter named Carole. "One of my earliest childhood memories," Carole recalls, "is of visiting George's grave." Carole explains her relationship with a man she never knew:

One day when I was very small visiting George's grave, I commented on how sad it was that George had died. Mom, being a mom, said that while it was very sad, if George hadn't died, I wouldn't have been born. In my childhood sensibility I explained...to her that yes I would, but my last name would have been Dancy! Just that simple. Always has been that simple...George Dancy has always been a part of my life. I have George's state police graduation picture on my desk. When someone wants to know why, I say it's my stepfather—it's just easier than explaining it all.[482]

George Richard Dancy has six grandchildren (all girls) and nine great-grandchildren. "George was all good," says his brother David. "A good brother, a good son, a good husband, a good father and I am sure a good trooper. Everybody liked George; some of us loved him."[483]

COURT

Finley Carl Fuchs #1435

Finley Carl Fuchs was born in Dunellen, New Jersey, on February 12, 1929, to John and Catherine Fuchs. When Finley was born, an economic storm was stirring, and by fall it arrived in the name of Black Tuesday. The Great Depression had begun. The surname Fuchs (pronounced Fooks) is of German descent, dating back to the medieval times in the area of Bavaria in Germany. During the mid-seventeenth century, the Fuchs began to immigrate to the United States. Catherine (née Flathery) was of Irish descent, and her maiden name is derived from the name Finonnlagh, meaning "white warrior."[484]

History has not recorded the early childhood of Finley Fuchs nor, in fact, much of his life altogether. The state police files are thin, with little substance on the man. Be that as it may, we are immediately thrust forward to his indoctrination into the New Jersey State Police.[485]

As a member of the forty-ninth state police class, Fuchs began training in May 1955 and endured a sixteen-week program of rigorous training. On August 19, Fuchs was one of forty-nine troopers graduating. The joyful occasion was met with a ninety-degree sun baking down on family and friends as they watched the celebration.[486]

Finley Fuchs's sojourn in the "outfit" began with an assignment to Troop C (central Jersey). He began his first patrol out of the Riverton Station, where Trooper George Dancy #1481 would also work. By November 1956, Fuchs was patrolling out of the Laurelton Station. Jersey troopers are initially hired under a two-year enlistment and, if eligible, reenlist for another two-

Finley Carl Fuchs #1435.

year period. Afterward, they are granted tenure. This practice is still in effect today. Fuchs completed his first enlisted period on August 19, 1957. His second enlistment had him working in Troop C Headquarters due to an injury he sustained. The nature of this injury isn't known.[487]

When Trooper Fuchs began his patrol on November 18, 1957, there was a bright blue sky shining down on him, and he was looking forward to coming to work, as he had returned to full duty. Now patrolling out of the Princeton Station, things were also shining brightly on his personal life. He was living at 134 Dunellen Avenue in Dunellen with his grandmother. Fuchs was very close with her and took good care of her. Moreover, he had met a woman named Florence Hegan, and the two fell in love and set a wedding date of Sunday, January 5, 1958.[488]

As the Christmas season was approaching, Fuchs had been hard at work in and around the historic town of Princeton. On December 18, 1957, at 10:00 a.m., he was investigating a motor vehicle accident involving a Princeton woman named Jane Rampona. For reasons never determined, Fuchs didn't conclude his investigation until the following day.[489]

The next day, Fuchs was back on patrol and looking forward to spending time with his fiancée when he got off duty. However, he had several court cases hanging over his head in the town of Laurelton. Court wasn't scheduled until after his shift, so near the end of his patrol, he stopped at the station, wrapped up his paperwork and spoke with John Smith #803, who was the station commander. When Smith heard that Fuchs planned on attending court in his personal vehicle, he suggested the trooper take a troop car instead. Fuchs appreciated the gesture but told his boss that he wanted to get right home after court.[490]

At 5:20 p.m., Fuchs was signed out of the station with the remarks, "Trooper Fuchs out, duty leave, to return 8:00 A.M., December 21, 1957." While en route to court, Fuchs stopped at the home of Jane Rampona, arriving at the home on Jefferson Road in Princeton about half past six o'clock. Fuchs had determined that Rampona was at fault for the previous day's accident and wrote her a summons. Getting into his own vehicle, he continued on his way to Laurelton Court. Interestingly, the three cases he had on the court calendar were for tickets relating to unsafe operation leading to a motor vehicle accident. While driving to court, Fuchs's operation of his own vehicle caused an accident that claimed his life.[491]

While traveling north on Route 9 in Freehold, Fuchs, for reasons unknown, entered into the southbound lane and struck a vehicle. The three occupants of the car received minor injuries, but the impact crushed the trooper's chest and ruptured his spleen. Finley Fuchs died at Fitkin Hospital in Neptune shortly after receiving last rites by a Roman Catholic priest.[492]

John and Catherine Fuchs were distraught at the loss of their child. For Florence, it was the end of her dream to be with the man she loved. However, the one most affected by his loss was his grandmother, Susan Flathery, who suffered a severe heart attack the day after Christmas.[493]

MYSTERY

Ronald E. Gray #1534

R onald Eugene Gray was born on June 29, 1935, in Hackensack, New Jersey. His parents, Albert and Frances Gray, must have been surprised because they got two for the price of one: Ronald was a twin to Albert Jr. Albert Dewitt Sr. was of English descent, and he and Frances resided in Rutherford, which is a suburb in Bergen County. At this time in their life, unemployment was over 19 percent. The Great Depression was a terribly difficult time for families such as the Grays. However, it is believed that Albert was able to maintain work as an employee for the Manhattan Rubber Company. The Rubber Company, located in the nearby city of Passaic, supported many workers in and around the Bergen County area. A few years later, Frances gave birth to another son, Glenn. The Gray children attended the public school system in the borough, and Ronald Gray received his high school diploma in June 1953.[494]

By 1953, Ronald had grown into a man of six feet, four inches and weighed nearly two hundred pounds. He had a ruddy complexion with brown hair and hazel eyes. The summer of 1953 was the last summer he would have free of any obligations; Gray enlisted in the United States Marine Corps, and on Monday, August 24, he was officially inducted as a U.S. Marine. During his tour, Gray served with the Marine Air Wing, rising in rank to a sergeant. In August 1956, Gray concluded his military career, being awarded an honorable discharge.[495]

While in the service, his family moved to 439 Washington Street in Carlstadt. Carlstadt, although twice as large in landmass as Rutherford, had

Ronald E. Gray #1534.

far fewer residents. When Gray returned from the military, he stayed with his parents and enrolled at Rutgers University.[496]

While in college, Gray applied to the New Jersey State Police along with his twin brother. On Sunday, March 24, 1957, at the age of twenty-one, the brothers began their training. The Grays entered the organization during a time of expansion, both in size and responsibility. During the 1950s, the New Jersey Turnpike and the Garden State Parkway opened, increasing the organization's patrol duties. Furthermore, the authority and responsibility of the organization was expanded into regulatory laws and oversight of security operations at the state capital.[497]

State Trooper Ronald Gray reported at 9:00 a.m. on Monday, July 15, to Troop B Headquarters for his assignment. By 1958, Ronald had met a woman, Marilyn Playfair, from Harrisburg, Pennsylvania. The two were wed on Monday, July 14, 1958, and the newlywed couple moved to Denville in Morris County. Considered the "hub" of Morris County, Denville is surrounded by several major thoroughfares.[498]

In light of the lack of documentation on Gray's service with the state police, and no firsthand accounts provided by family members, we are moved forward to November 1958, when Gray was on patrol out of the

Newton Station in Sussex County.[499] The Newton State Police Station was located on Route 202, and troopers working here provided police services to many towns in the area. To this day, towns such as Green, Lafayette, Hampton, Fredon, Swartswood, Stillwater and Andover still have Jersey troopers patrolling their communities. In 1986, the Newton Station and the Hainsville Station were merged to form what is today the Sussex Station.[500]

The warm days of the summer had faded into the cold fall weather. On Thursday, November 27, Ronald and Marilyn celebrated their first Thanksgiving together. As is the life of a trooper, Gray was back to work during the holiday weekend. On November 30, 1958, Gray reported for

Trooper Gray. *Unknown newspaper photo.*

duty. It was a bitterly cold day, with the nighttime temperature lingering around eighteen degrees. For this night's shift, Gray was partnered with Trooper Robert Ziegler #1387. As the night rolled on, midnight had come and gone and it was now the early morning hours of December 1. About 2:15 a.m., Gray and Ziegler were driving south on Route 206 in the town of Andover. What happened next was headlined in the next day's paper: "2 Hurt; Mystery Surrounds Mishap." At the age of twenty-three, after less than a year as a trooper, Gray's life had been taken. This incident left state police officials puzzled as to what had caused the wreck. What is known is that Gray's state police cruiser struck a concrete bridge abutment. According to the local newspaper, the vehicle "just flew apart." Victor Brown was sleeping in his home when he heard the loud crash. His account was included in the newspaper: "It was the worst thing I've ever seen," said Brown. A local doctor was summoned to the scene and, after taking Gray's vitals, pronounced him dead. The accident was a gruesome sight that left Gray's body lodged in the wreckage and ejected Ziegler from the vehicle. It was a miracle that Ziegler was not also killed. Records do not say whether Ziegler ever clarified what occurred on that fateful night.[501]

Ronald Gray was buried at the George Washington Memorial Cemetery in Paramus, New Jersey, leaving behind his parents, two brothers and his wife, Marilyn.[502]

On January 15, 1959, Marilyn Gray revealed that she was pregnant. Sadly, on Wednesday, June 17, Marilyn's child was stillborn. This is a sad postscript to the story of Ronald Gray.[503]

MOTORIST AID

Hilary Welenc #1190

In 1676, the Leni-Lenape Indians sold thirty miles of Delaware River front land to proprietors seeking to live in the region known today as Burlington. In the eighteenth century, Burlington resident John Lawrence rose to become mayor of Burlington and a state assemblyman. However, during the American Revolution, Lawrence was loyal to Britain and was forced out of power. His son James had a greater contribution to America as the navy commander whose dying command was "Don't give up the ship." The nexus that Burlington has with the New Jersey State Police is a man named Hilary Welenc.[504]

Hilary Welenc's mother and father were Polish immigrants; his mother, Maryanna (née Szewczykowska), was born on June 23, 1891, and his father, Teofil, was born in Placko, Poland, on June 27, 1885. While in Poland, Teofil worked as a molder molding iron, brass and other materials. On June 18, 1905, he arrived in America, where he met Maryanna. The couple married and had three girls—Mary, Jenny and Cecilia—before Hilary was born on January 14, 1929. All four children were born in their home at 126 Delaware Avenue. Their house sat right on the riverbank. (Today, this location is a park.) When Hilary was one year old, his father Teofil caught pneumonia and died at the age of forty-five.[505]

Maryanna raised her children alone, supporting her family by working in the Peerless Dress Factory in Burlington. (Sadly, Maryanna would see Mary and Hilary precede her in death.) Larry, as friends and family called him, attended All Saints School in Burlington. To be a student there, one had

Hilary Welenc #1190. *Courtesy of Sandra Pennipede.*

to have a Polish parent or grandparent. All through school, Larry received his education in the Polish language. Accordingly, he wrote and spoke the language fluently. After graduating, Larry attended the local high school, where he became a member of the Movie Operator Club, the Camera Club and the Sports Review Club.[506]

After Larry's older sister Mary and her husband Peter Yuengling married in 1939, they moved into the Welenc Delaware Avenue home. Mary and Peter had a daughter named Mary Ann, and Larry took good care of his little niece. The Welenc household has been described as an "old world Euroupean atmosphere." As Larry took on the big brother role, so did Peter Yuengling. Peter bought Larry his first bicycle and roller skates and became Welenc's mentor. Peter was a police officer in Burlington who rose through the ranks to become the police chief. Interestingly, Welenc's sister Jenny married a police officer who also became a police chief in the nearby town of Riverside. The police influence was strong in the Welenc household, but Peter's influence was the most profound on the young man.[507]

In June 1947, Larry graduated from Burlington High School. On that same day, another graduating student named Angie Ruggeri found a nearly new notebook bearing the name of someone she was not familiar with: Larry Welenc. She thought nothing of it and kept the book.[508]

Larry Welenc had entertained aspirations of becoming an engineer but didn't have money to pursue this course of study. Larry had a conversation with his mother and Peter, and they collectively determined that the military was the best choice for him. On July 8, 1947, approximately a month after his graduation, Welenc joined the United States Air Force, enlisting for three years. He served his tour in Guam and was discharged as a corporal on July 7, 1950.[509]

After leaving the service, Welenc began working at the Riverside Metal Company in Riverside, New Jersey, as a time study analyst. About this time, that teenager who had found Larry's notebook a few years prior finally got to meet the man named on the cover. Angeline "Angie" was born on January 3, 1929, and grew up in the neighboring town of Beverly. Her parents, Antonio Ruggeri and Antonia (née Gringeri), Italian immigrants, raised six children together. It is amazing that throughout school, Angie's and Larry's paths never crossed; the two quickly became inseparable. They were engaged in May 1952, and shortly thereafter, the influence that Larry's brothers-in-law had on him was manifested in his application to the New Jersey State Police.[510]

Welenc began training on Sunday, August 17, 1952, as a member of the forty-second class. The academy training was residential and required little time for visiting his family. On Sundays, Peter would pile everyone in the car to visit Larry at the academy. Mary Ann Yuengling remembers these visits fondly, as she was full of pride.[511]

On November 26, 1952, after an intense training program, Larry graduated with 51 other men. The process was finally complete. It had begun with 964 people taking the test and had been narrowed to those 51 members graduating—the few who had earned the right to be called a Jersey trooper.[512] The forty-second class brought the "outfit" up to 614 troopers strong. Trooper Welenc was assigned to the Woodstown Station. Eventually, he was transferred to the Morrestown Station on the New Jersey Turnpike in 1954.[513]

In addition to his trooper obligations, Welenc was also a member of the Burlington Lodge No. 996 and the Italian American Club. He enjoyed public service and was a volunteer fireman at the Hope Fire Company. Meanwhile, Angie worked as a secretary for the Rheem Manufacturing Company in Burlington and the A.F. Holden Company in Mount Holly, New Jersey. After

Standing proud. *Courtesy of Sandra Pennipede.*

marrying, the couple lived at 401B Lawrence Street in Burlington. On July 12, 1957, their son Larry Michael was born. A year later, on November 8, 1958, their daughter Sandra Jean followed. When his children were born, Welenc said that he was going to spend as much time with his children as possible so they would know what it was like to have a father, something that he had longed for as a child. And every breathing minute of his life, he held true to his declaration.[514]

As a trooper, Welenc learned his job well and developed a keen sense for deviant behavior. In essence, he had a cop's intuition.[515]

Monday, February 1, 1954, was a bitterly cold day as Welenc reported to the Moorstown Station to begin his New Jersey Turnpike assignment. It is well known that riffraff travel this main artery into New York running illicit drugs, guns and illegal contraband. Furthermore, the sheer volume of traffic traversing the road makes a turnpike assignment dangerous work. Welenc's police skills and his "intuition" are highlighted by the number of criminal arrests he had out on what troopers call "the Black Dragon." Highlighting his skills are the events of July 18, 1955. It was a beautiful summer's day, and Larry was out on patrol when he stopped a vehicle for a minor infraction. Soon, he realized that the occupants were up to no good and took quick action, arresting the occupants and recovering a loaded handgun. Another such illustration of his abilities occurred on August 11, 1955, when he stopped a car that had been stolen out of New York City.[516]

While patrolling the turnpike, Welenc encountered many situations, some horrible and others amusing. On one occasion, the young trooper stopped a Polish couple who proceeded to badmouth the trooper in their native tongue, not knowing that he, too, spoke Polish. Welenc thought this amusing and let them have their conversation. After they were done, he told them in Polish that he understood their frustration but was just enforcing the law. Luckily for them, Welenc was compassionate and released them with a warning. Another interesting incident is when the bus carrying the Brooklyn Dodgers to the 1956 World Series against the Philadelphia Phillies broke down. Welenc was able to expedite a bus to their location and sent them on their way. For his efforts, the whole team signed a baseball for him. That baseball bears the names of Sandy Koufax, Roy Campanella, Don Drysdale and Jackie Robinson.[517]

Sadly, these "turnpike stories" are overshadowed by the events of Friday, November 20, 1959, when Trooper Welenc entered troop car #47 and began his shift. While patrolling southbound on the turnpike, Welenc passed the spot where Sergeant Frank Trainor had been struck and killed just a few years earlier. Farther down the highway, Welenc came upon a motorist who was changing a flat tire with a man, two women and a child standing on the shoulder. Trooper Welenc pulled his black-and-white behind the man and turned on his overhead emergency light.[518]

The driver, a sixty-six-year-old man, had been traveling with his wife and their friends when the tire went flat. The motorist pulled his vehicle to the shoulder at mile post 31. Welenc offered a hand, and the two began taking the spare out of the trunk. While they were standing between the troop car and disabled vehicle, a truck struck the back of the troop car, sending it forward and crushing Welenc and the man. Both men died as a result of their injuries. When asked by investigators what had happened, the driver simply said, "I fell asleep."[519]

One of Mary Ann's most treasured memories is of when she, her dad and Uncle Larry would sit in the kitchen and spend hours talking. In her eighteen years of life, Mary Ann never saw her father cry, but when he was told of Larry's death, he went up to his room by himself and could be heard weeping. [520]

The funeral for Trooper Welenc was held on Tuesday, November 24, at the W.H. Page Funeral Home in Burlington. It was the biggest funeral Burlington had ever witnessed. Hilary Welenc was buried at the Odd Fellows Cemetery in Burlington. Angeline Welenc never remarried and died in 2004. Hilary "Larry" Welenc's legacy includes two grandsons, Nicolas and Dante.[521]

NOTES

BLOOD POISONING

1. Newark City, NJ website. http://www.ci.newark.nj.us.
2. William H. Marshall New Jersey State Police (NJSP) Museum file.
3. Ibid. Marshall's application says that he was a Silver Star winner. However, records indicate that the Silver Star did not yet exist for World War I.
4. Leo Coakley, *Jersey Troopers* (Piscataway, NJ: Rutgers University Press, 1971); Marshall NJSP Museum file.
5. Ibid.
6. NJSP official website, www.njsp.org; Marshall NJSP Museum file.
7. Ibid.
8. Ibid.
9. Ibid.
10. Captain Othel Baxter letter, July 8, 1922.
11. Ibid.
12. Ibid.
13. Ibid.

MURDER AT CHIMNEY ROCK

14. Robert E. Coyle NJSP Museum file; Coyle genealogy raw data, http://freepages.genealogy.rootsweb.com.
15. Ibid.
16. Ibid.
17. Ibid.
18. NJSP teletype #63, December 19, 1924; *Newark Evening News*, February 9, 1925; *New York Times*, December 19, 1924, and December 21, 1924. Another newspaper article claims that the troopers saw Genese walking down the road and, after delivering the money, went back to confront him. While doing so, they were ambushed by three

other men, along with Genese. This newspaper account (unknown paper) has many inconsistencies and errors contained in it, and this author deems this information unreliable.

19. Ibid.
20. Ibid.
21. Ibid.
22. Ibid.
23. Ibid.
24. Ibid.
25. NJSP official website, www.njsp.org.
26. *New York Times*, December 19, 1924, and December 21, 1924.
27. Ibid.
28. *Newark Evening News*, Monday February 9, 1925; *New York Times*, December 19, 1924, and December 21, 1924.
29. Ibid.
30. Ibid.
31. Ibid
32. Ibid.
33. Ibid.
34. Ibid.
35. Ibid.
36. Ibid.
37. Ibid.
38. John J. Coyle to Honorable George Silzer, February 10, 1925; *Newark Evening News*, February 9, 1925; *New York Times*, December 19, 1924, and December 21, 1924.
39. Ibid.

Shooting at the Speakeasy

40. Oracle ThinkQuest Educational Foundation, "Prohibition—The 'Noble Experiment,'" http://library.thinkquest.org/04oct/00492; NJSP official website, www.njsp.org.
41. Charles Ullrich NJSP Museum file; "A History of Paterson," www.patersonnj.com; Survivors of the Triangle, "In Loving Memory Of…" www.survivorsofthetriangle.org/ullrich.html; Oracle ThinkQuest Educational Foundation, "Prohibition—The 'Noble Experiment,'" http://library.thinkquest.org/04oct/00492.
42. Ullrich NJSP Museum file.
43. Ibid.
44. Ibid.
45. Wikipedia, "List of United States Navy Ratings," http://en.wikipedia.org/wiki/List_of_United_States_Navy_ratings; Ullrich NJSP Museum file.
46. Ullrich NJSP Museum file.
47. Ibid.
48. NJSP official website, www.njsp.org.
49. Untitled and undated newspaper article from Ullrich NJSP Museum file.
50. Ibid.
51. Oracle ThinkQuest Educational Foundation, "Prohibition—The 'Noble Experiment,'" http://library.thinkquest.org/04oct/00492; *Newark Evening News*,

February 17, 1926; *New York Times*, February 18, 1926; NJSP official website, www. njsp.org.

52. Ibid.
53. Ibid.
54. Isabel Stephen, "Find the Girls from French Hill," *Official Detective Stories*, n.d.; *Newark Evening News*, February 17, 1926.
55. Ibid.
56. Ibid.
57. Ibid.
58. Ibid.
59. Ibid.
60. Ibid.
61. Ibid.
62. *Newark Evening News*, February 17, 1926; Stephen, "Find the Girls from French Hill."
63. Ibid.
64. *Newark Evening News*, February 17, 1926; Gerald Tomlinson, *Murdered in Jersey* (Piscataway, NJ: Rutgers University Press, 1994).
65. *Newark Evening News*, February, 17, 1926.

FORGOTTEN

66. *Paterson Evening Post*, May 9, 1926; Matthew Keegan, "Haledon, New Jersey: A Renaissance in the Making?" October 12, 2005, http://EzineArticles. com/?expert=Matthewkeegan; *Paterson Evening News*, May 14, 1926; American Meteorological Society, AMS Journals Online, http://ams.allenpress.com.
67. *Paterson Evening Post*, May 9, 1926; Keegan, "Haledon, New Jersey"; *Paterson Evening News*, May 14, 1926; Herman Gloor Jr. NJSP Museum file.
68. Ibid.
69. NJSP Special Order #270, May 10, 1926; Gloor NJSP Museum file.
70. Gloor NJSP Museum file.
71. Ibid.
72. Ibid.; Coyle NJSP Museum file.
73. Ibid.
74. NJSP Special Order #270, May 10, 1926.
75. Unknown newspaper, "Trooper Exonerated in Bribery Rumors," n.d.; *Paterson Evening News*, May 9, 1926; *Trenton Times*, May 13, 1926.
76. Ibid.
77. NJSP Special Order #270, May 10, 1926.
78. Ibid.
79. Paterson Evening News, n.d.; Gloor NJSP Museum file.
80. Lieutenant C.T. DeFeo to Major R.D. Bloom, 1993; Gloor NJSP Museum file.

VIEW OBSTRUCTION

81. NJSP Special Order #13, August 5, 1926; NJSP official website, njsp.org; Walter Arrowsmith NJSP Museum file; Wikipedia, "Lawrenceville, New Jersey," http://en.wikipedia.org/wiki/Lawrenceville,_NJLawrenceville.
82. Ibid.

83. Wikipedia, "Lawrenceville, New Jersey," http://en.wikipedia.org/wiki/Lawrenceville,_NJLawrenceville; unknown newspaper article, 1926.
84. NJSP Special Order #13, August 5, 1926; Wikipedia, "Lawrenceville, New Jersey," http://en.wikipedia.org/wiki/Lawrenceville,_NJLawrenceville.
85. NJSP Special Order #13, August 5, 1926; Matt Moffatt, "History of Ice Manufacturing at the Turn of the Twentieth Century," www.otal.umd.edu.
86. Unknown newspaper article, 1926.
87. NJSP Special Order #13, August 5, 1926; NJSP official website, www.njsp.org; unknown newspaper article, 1926.
88. Arrowsmith NJSP Museum file.
89. American Meteorological Society, AMS Journals Online, http://ams.allenpress.com.
90. Author's interpretation.
91. Trooper F.N. Pennal #275 Investigative Report, August 8, 1926; unknown newspaper article, 1926.
92. Ibid.
93. Ibid.
94. Ibid.
95. Ibid.
96. NJSP Special Order #13, August 5, 1926; unknown newspaper article, 1926.
97. Trooper F.N. Pennal #275 Investigative Report, August 8, 1926.
98. NJSP Special Order #13, August 5, 1926.

"Old Malady"
99. David Ernst NJSP Museum file; Waynesboro, PA, www.waynesboropa.org.
100. www.surnames.com.
101. *Newark Evening News*, August 5, 1927; Ernst NJSP Museum file; Lehigh Valley Railroad Historical Society, http://www.lvrrhs.org/history/index.htm.
102. Ernst NJSP Museum file.
103. Ibid.; Wikipedia, "South Plainfield, New Jersey," http://en.wikipedia.org/wiki/South_Plainfield,_NJ.
104. *Newark Evening News*, August 5, 1927; Ernst NJSP Museum file.
105. Ibid.
106. Ibid.
107. Ibid.
108. Ibid.
109. Ibid.

Adopted
110. Joseph A. Smith NJSP Museum file. Note: NJSP Special Order #10, dated August 6, 1927, states Smith's rank as a sergeant. However, he was actually a second lieutenant.
111. *Asbury Park Press*, August 6, 1927.
112. Ibid.
113. Smith NJSP Museum file.
114. *Asbury Park Press*, August 6, 1927.
115. Ibid.
116. Ibid.; Smith NJSP Museum file.

COLD-BLOODED MURDER

117. *State Police Magazine*, n.d.

118. Wikipedia, "Stanhope, New Jersey," http://en.wikipedia.org/wiki/Stanhope,_ New_Jersey; Canal Society of New Jersey, www.canalsocietynj.org; Peter Gladys NJSP Museum file.

119. *New Jersey Herald*, January 3, 1929; Gladys NJSP Museum file.

120. *New Jersey Herald*, January 3, 1929; *Trenton Times*, December 29, 1928.

121. NJSP official website, www.njsp.org.

122. *New Jersey Herald*, January 3, 1929; *Trenton Times*, December 29, 1928.

123. Ibid.

124. Wikipedia, "Allentown, New Jersey," http://en.wikipedia.org/wiki/Allentown,_ NJ; author's interpretation.

125. *New Jersey Herald*, January 3, 1929; *Trenton Times*, December 29, 1928.

126. Chas. H. Schoeffel to Colonel H. Normal Schwarzkopf, January 11, 1929; *New Jersey Herald*, January 3, 1929; *Trenton Times*, December 29, 1928.

127. Ibid.

128. Ibid.

129. Ibid.

130. Ibid.; *The Bee* [Danville, VA], December 31, 1928.

131. Gladys NJSP Museum file.

132. R.A. Snook, "Negro's Trial Ends Abruptly: Alienists to Pass on Trooper's Slayer," *State Trooper Magazine*, n.d.

UNDOCUMENTED

133. ePodunk, "Shenandoah, Pennsylvania," http://www.epodunk.com/cgi-bin/ genInfo.php?locIndex=14835; Wikipedia, "Shenandoah, Pennsylvania," http:// en.wikipedia.org/wiki/Shenandoah,_PA.

134. Ibid.

135. 1890 Federal Census Directory Report.

136. NJSP teletype #84, March 5, 1929; www.surnames.com.

137. NJSP teletype #84, March 5, 1929.

138. M.O. Kimberling to superintendent, April 8, 1929.

139. Wikipedia, "Deerfield Township, New Jersey," http://en.wikipedia.org/wiki/ Deerfield_Township,_New_Jersey; ePodunk, "Deerfield, New Jersey," http://www. epodunk.com/cgi-bin/genInfo.php?locIndex=18038.

140. Ibid.

141. NJSP official website, www.njsp.org; author's interpretation.

142. Ibid.

143. NJSP teletype #84, March 5, 1929; *Morristown Daily Record*, March 1, 1929.

144. Ibid.

INFECTION

145. John Divers NJSP Museum file; ePodunk, "Blairstown, New Jersey," http://www. epodunk.com/cgi-bin/genInfo.php?locIndex=18721.

146. Wikipedia, "Columbia, New Jersey," http://en.wikipedia.org/wiki/Columbia,_NJ; www.epodunk.com; Ernst NJSP Museum file.

147. Ernst NJSP Museum file.

148. Divers NJSP Museum file; Wikipedia, "World War I," http://en.wikipedia.org/wiki/World_war_i.

149. Ibid.

150. NJSP official website, www.njsp.org.

151. Divers NJSP Museum file.

152. Ibid.

153. *Trenton Times*, May 13, 1926; NJSP Special Order #69.

154. NJSP Special Order #217, December 24, 1929.

155. Captain Frank Gilbert to NJSP, March 6, 1930; Captain W.O. Nicol to H. Norman Schwarzkopf, March 11, 1930; David Hackett Fischer, *Washington's Crossing* (New York: Oxford University Press, 2004): 420, 576.

156. Gilbert to NJSP, March 6, 1930.

157. Ibid.

158. Ibid.

159. Ibid.

160. A.H. Roberts, MD, to the Board of Health of Burlington, September 9, 1929.

161. Captain W.O. Nicol to H. Norman Schwarzkopf, March 11, 1930.

162. Ibid.

163. Telegram sent by H. Norman Schwarzkopf to Superintendent Easton Hospital, April 22, 1930.

164. Divers NJSP Museum file.

Caution

165. NJSP teletype, March 4, 1931.

166. NJSP teletype, March 5, 1931; *Perth Amboy Evening News*, March 5, 1931 (this paper lists his year of birth as 1907, with the age of twenty-three at his death); Wikipedia, "Perth Amboy, New Jersey," http://en.wikipedia.org/wiki/Perth_Amboy,_New_Jersey.

167. *Perth Amboy Evening News*, March 5, 1931.

168. Ibid.; Peter W. Ignatz NJSP Museum file.

169. NJSP teletype, March 5, 1931.

170. Ibid.

171. *Hunterdon County Democrat*, "Trooper Injured Avoiding Crash," n.d.

172. Ibid.

173. Unsigned letter to Colonel H. Norman Schwarzkopf, December 8, 1930; *Hunterdon County Democrat*, "Trooper Injured Avoiding Crash," n.d.

174. *Hunterdon County Democrat*, "Trooper Injured Avoiding Crash," n.d.; *Morristown Daily Record*, March 5, 1931.

175. *Morristown Daily Record*, March 5, 1931. The troop cycle that Ignatz was driving had New Jersey license plate G6324; Commercial Casualty Insurance Company, Report of Automobile Accident, March 8, 1931.

176. *Morristown Daily Record*, March 5, 1931; NJSP teletype, March 5, 1931; *Perth Amboy Evening News*, March 5, 1931.

177. Ibid.

Allegations

178. NJSP Special Order #180, June 29, 1931; www.surnames.com.

179. Leonard McCandless NJSP Museum file.

180. NJSP Special Order #180, June 29, 1931. The stock market crashed on Tuesday, October 29, 1929.

181. Leonard McCandless NJSP Museum file; Ernest Cotterell to H. Normal Schwarzkopf, October 19, 1931.

182. McCandless NJSP Museum file.

183. Ibid.

184. Captain H.F. Wooge to H. Norman Schwarzkopf, July 21, 1931; Percy Camp to Mr. Geo. P. Seebaeck et al., June 29, 1931; Captain H.F. Wooge to H. Norman Schwarzkopf, July 28, 1931; Captain H.F. Wooge to H. Norman Schwarzkopf, July 27, 1931; NJSP accident report authored by Trooper E.O. Hetterman #488, June 28, 1931.

185. Ibid.

186. Ibid.

187. NJSP Special Order #180, June 29, 1931.

188. McCandless NJSP Museum file.

HIT AND RUN

189. Beylon was born in Philadelphia; however, it is a presumption that the Beylon family was living there. This is based on the fact that Elizabeth had hospitals just as capable as Philadelphia to deliver children; in turn, the Beylons lived in or around the Philadelphia area. Michael Beylon NJSP Museum file; interview with Robert Vargus (Beylon), Michael Beylon's son.

190. Ibid.

191. Interview with Robert Vargus (Beylon); interview with Betty Beylon, Michael Beylon's sister; "A History of the Standard Oil Company," www.us-highways.com/sohist.htm; Beylon NJSP Museum file.

192. Interview with Betty Beylon.

193. Beylon NJSP Museum file.

194. Interview with Robert Vargus (Beylon); Beylon NJSP Museum file.

195. Beylon NJSP Museum file.

196. Interview with Robert Vargus (Beylon) Beylon's son; interview with Betty Beylon; charge sheet, October 10, 1930; Beylong NJSP Museum file; interview statement of Marion L. Ballis, February 24, 1932.

197. Ibid.

198. Ibid.

199. Ibid.

200. Ibid.

201. Ibid.

202. Ibid.

203. Ibid.

204. Ibid.

205. Interview with Robert Vargus (Beylon).

TROOPER AND THE MYSTERY WOMAN

206. John Ressler NJSP Museum file; www.brainyhistory.com.

207. Wikipedia, "Newark, New Jersey," http://en.wikipedia.org/wiki/Newark,_nj Newark; Wikipedia, "Hillside, New Jersey," http://en.wikipedia.org/wiki/Hillside,_NJ; Ressler NJSP Museum file; www.brainyhistory.com.

208. Ressler NJSP Museum file; www.brainyhistory.com.
209. Ibid.
210. Corporal A.T. Wilhelm to Captain W.J. Carter, December 16, 1930. The accident occurred on December 16, 1930, at the intersection of Egg Harbor Road and Seventh Street in Mays Landing.
211. Ressler NJSP Museum file.
212. NJSP accident report, May 1, 1932; NJSP teletype, May 1, 1932.
213. Ibid.

LIFEGUARD

214. ePodunk, "Belmar, New Jersey," http://www.epodunk.com/cgi-bin/genInfo. php?locIndex=18292; Wikipedia, "Belmar, New Jersey," http://en.wikipedia.org/ wiki/Belmar,_NJ; James Herbert NJSP Museum file.
215. Special report of investigation by Corporal J.J. McCormack #330, March 15, 1931.
216. Ibid.
217. Herbert NJSP Museum file; unknown newspaper article, n.d.
218. Beylon NJSP Museum file; Ressler NJSP Museum file; NJSP Museum files on the Lindbergh investigation; unknown newspaper article, n.d.
219. Author's personal knowledge of Pompton Lakes, Wayne Township and the old Pompton Lakes Barracks, which today is a store.
220. Unknown newspaper article, n.d.; Coakley, *Jersey Troopers*.
221. NJSP teletype, July 9, 1932; author's personal knowledge of Wayne Township and the old swimming pond that was located near Hinchman Road in Wayne.
222. Special report of investigation by Corporal J.J. McCormack #330, March 15, 1931.
223. NJSP Special Order #136, July 11, 1932. Note: The investigation report authored by Corporal J.J. McCormack #330 mentions a "side road." That road today is Hinchman Road.

FOG

224. James Scotland NJSP Museum file; Wikipedia, "Glasgow, Scotland," http:// en.wikipedia.org/wiki/Glasgow,_Scotland; untitled newspaper obituary of James Scotland, n.d.
225. Scotland NJSP Museum file; Marshall NJSP Museum file.
226. Scotland NJSP Museum file; "Old Nutley," www.oldnutley.org.
227. Scotland NJSP Museum file.
228. Untitled newspaper obituary of James Scotland, n.d.; Wikipedia, "Vaudeville," http://en.wikipedia.org/wiki/Vaudeville; interview with Virginia Scotland (sister-in-law), February 19, 2008.
229. NJSP official website, www.njsp.org; Former Troopers Association, *New Jersey State Police 75-Year History* (Trenton, NJ: self-published, 1995).
230. *Trenton Times*, February 19, 1935; untitled newspaper obituary of James Scotland, n.d.
231. S.H. Conover to Colonel Schwarzkopf, September 22, 1933.
232. Ibid.
233. *Trenton Times*, February 19, 1935; NJSP official website, www.njsp.org, see John Divers chapter.

234. *Trenton Times*, February 19, 1935.

235. NJSP Special Order #347, February 19, 1935.

ROBBERY AND MURDER

236. Interview with Donna Dawes Yenser; Warren Yenser NJSP Museum file.

237. Ibid.

238. Untitled magazine article, July 4, 1929, contained in Yenser NJSP Museum file.

239. Ibid.

240. Yenser NJSP Museum file.

241. Iris Rose Bogorad to Warren G. Yenser, August 3, 1934; Yenser NJSP Museum file; Joseph Mittutoheon to Warren G. Yenser, n.d.

242. Interview with Donna Dawes Yenser; notes written by Warren G. Yenser, January 22, 1935.

243. Iris Rose Bogorad to Warren G. Yenser, August 3, 1934.

244. Interview with Donna Dawes Yenser; unnamed and undated newspaper article of the Yenser/Blair wedding.

245. Notes written by Warren G. Yenser, June 18, 1935.

246. Interview with Donna Dawes Yenser; notes written by Warren G. Yenser, June 18, 1935.

247. *Newark Evening News*, November 9, 1935; autopsy report of Warren G. Yenser.

248. Ibid.

249. Ibid.

250. Dorothy E. Yenser to Colonel H. Norman Schwarzkopf, November 13, 1935.

251. *Newark Evening News*, November 9, 1935.

252. Colonel H. Norman Schwarzkopf, NJSP General Order #1; *Newark Evening News*, November 9, 1935.

253. *Newark Evening News*, November 9, 1935.

254. Interview with Hugo Stockburger Badge #504, retired major, NJSP; *Newark Evening News*, November 9, 1935.

255. Ibid.

256. Interview with Donna Dawes Yenser.

THE MODEL TROOPER

257. *Trenton Times*, June 14, 1937.

258. Interview with Barbara (Perry) Adams, February 22, 2008.

259. Ibid.

260. Former Troopers Association, *New Jersey State Police 75-Year History*; interview with Barbara (Perry) Adams, February 22, 2008.

261. Interview with Barbara (Perry) Adams, February 22, 2008.

262. Ibid.; NJSP Special Order #162, June 9, 1931; Former Troopers Association, *New Jersey State Police 75-Year History*.

263. Interview with Barbara (Perry) Adams, February 22, 2008.

264. NJSP accident report authored by Corporal S. Polkowitz #566, June 7, 1937; NJSP official website, www.njsp.org.

265. Ibid.

266. *Vineland Evening News*, June, 9, 1937; NJSP Special Order #543, June 9, 1931.

267. Ibid.

268. Interview with Barbara (Perry) Adams, February 22, 2008.

STRUGGLE FOR A STRONG MAN

269. Interview with Ann McManus, January 27, 2009.

270. Ibid.

271. Ibid.; Chas. H. Schoeffel to Dr. Marcus A. Curry, December 27, 1935.

272. Ibid.

273. Ibid.

274. Ibid.

275. Ibid.

276. Ibid.

277. Ibid.

278. Ibid.

279. Dr. Mills private hospital letter, February 12, 1938; Dr. Mills private hospital letter, n.d.

280. Matthew McManus NJSP Museum file; Dr. Mills private hospital letter, February 12, 1938; Dr. Mills private hospital letter, n.d.

281. NJSP *Triangle*, "Sergeant Ryan and Trooper McManus Have Narrow Escape."

282. Interview with Ann McManus, January 27, 2009.

283. Matthew M. McManus letter, March 5, 1927.

284. Interview with Ann McManus, January 27, 2009; Dr. Mills private hospital letter, February 12, 1938; Dr. Mills private hospital letter, n.d.; Chas. H. Schoeffel to Dr. Marcus A. Curry, December 27, 1935.

285. Interview with Ann McManus, January 27, 2009.

286. Dr. Mills private hospital letter, February 12, 1938; Dr. Mills private hospital letter, n.d.

287. NJSP Teletype Message #B-206, February 28, 1938.

LONG RIDE

288. NJSP Special Order #633.

289. Ibid.; History of Jersey City, www.cityofjerseycity.com.

290. NJSP Special Order #633.

291. Ibid.

292. Former Troopers Association, *New Jersey State Police 75-Year History*; Colonel Mark Kimberling to Vincent C. Vosbein, May 17, 1937.

293. NJSP Special Order #633.

294. Ibid.; NJSP official website, www.njsp.org.

295. Former Troopers Association, *New Jersey State Police 75-Year History*.

296. NJSP Special Order #633.

297. Ibid.

298. Corporal A. Bencer #316, report, June 18, 1938.

299. Ibid.

300. NJSP Special Order #633.

301. Ibid.

ICE AND THE JENNY JUMP

302. NJSP Special Order #783, January 25, 1940; NJSP Special Order #666, November 14, 1938; ePodunk, "Hoboken, New Jersey," http://www.epodunk.com/cgi-bin/genInfo.php?locIndex=18551.

303. Interview with Peter Ardito (nephew).

304. Ibid.

305. NJSP Special Order #783, January 25, 1940; NJSP Special Order #666, November 14, 1938. ePodunk, "Hoboken, New Jersey," http://www.epodunk.com/cgi-bin/genInfo.php?locIndex=18551; interview with Peter Ardito.

306. Ibid.

307. Ibid.

308. NJSP Blairstown teletype, January 24, 1940; NJSP headquarters teletype to Trans Radio Press, January 24, 1940.

309. NJSP Special Order #783, January 25, 1940.

310. Ibid.; NJSP Special Order #666, November 14, 1938; NJSP Morristown Headquarters teletype #A-17, January 3, 1939; Lieutenant Harry A. Cibulla to Captain William O. Nicol, January, 24, 1940.

311. Ibid.

312. Ibid.

313. NJSP Special Order #783, January 25, 1940; NJSP Special Order #666, November 14, 1938.

314. Ibid.

AVIATION

315. NJSP teletype, April 29, 1941; ePodunk, "Trenton, New Jersey," http://www.epodunk.com/cgi-bin/genInfo.php?locIndex=18303.

316. NJSP teletype, April 29, 1941; Wikipedia, "Trenton-Mercer Airport," http://en.wikipedia.org/wiki/Trenton-Mercer_Airport.

317. NJSP teletype, April 29, 1941; Boy Scout Troop 15, http://mysite.verizon.net/troop15.

318. NJSP teletype, April 29, 1941; Wikipedia, "Trenton-Mercer Airport," http://en.wikipedia.org/wiki/Trenton-Mercer_Airport.

319. NJSP teletype, April 29, 1941; NJSP Special Order #705, April 28, 1939.

320. NJSP teletype, April 29, 1941; NJSP Special Order #705, April 28, 1939.

321. Aviation Hall of Fame & Museum of New Jersey, www.njahof.org; NJSP official website, www.njsp.org; NJSP teletype, April 29, 1941; NJSP Special Order #705, April 28, 1939.

322. John Gregerson NJSP Museum file.

323. Ibid.

324. Ibid.

325. Gregerson NJSP Museum file; Aviation Hall of Fame & Museum of New Jersey, www.njahof.org.

326. Interview with William Baldwin, April 7, 2006; Gregerson NJSP Museum file.

327. Norman K. Karn to Colonel Kimberling, May 2, 1941; Gill R. Wilson to Colonel Mark Kimberling, May 5, 1941; Captain Walter J. Coughlin to "The Superintendent," April 18, 1941.

328. Gill R. Wilson to Colonel Mark Kimberling, May 5, 1941.

329. NJSP teletype, April 29, 1941.

330. Gill R. Wilson to Colonel Mark Kimberling, May 5, 1941.

331. NJSP teletype, April 29, 1941.

THE FRUIT STAND

332. William J. Doolan NJSP Museum file; ePodunk, "Bayonne New Jersey," http://www.epodunk.com/cgi-bin/genInfo.php?locIndex=18510.

333. Doolan NJSP Museum file.

334. NJSP Special Order #59, October 15, 1942.

335. Former Troopers Association, *New Jersey State Police 75-Year History*; Aviation Hall of Fame & Museum of New Jersey, www.njahof.org.

336. Ibid.

337. Doolan NJSP Museum file.

338. J.J. Harris to Captain Daniel J. Dunn, October 23, 1944.

339. Ibid.

340. Ibid.

341. Ibid.

342. Doolan NJSP Museum file.

WHERE OTHERS WOULD NOT GO

343. Francis R. O'Brien NJSP Museum file; interview with Francis W. O'Brien; interview with Keith O'Brien.

344. Ibid.

345. Ibid.

346. Ibid.

347. Former Troopers Association, *New Jersey State Police 75-Year History*.

348. O'Brien NJSP Museum file; interview with Francis W. O'Brien; interview with Keith O'Brien; ePodunk, "Port Norris, New Jersey," http://www.epodunk.com/cgi-bin/genInfo.php?locIndex=296417.

349. *Publican* newspaper, n.d.; O'Brien NJSP Museum file.

350. Ibid.

351. Colonel Chas. H. Schoeffel to commanding officer, Troop A, August 7, 1936; Captain W.J. Carter to Colonel Chas. H Schoeffel, April 21, 1939; Samuel B. English, MD, to Major Mark O. Kimberling, April 27, 1939; *Publican* newspaper, n.d.

352. Interview with Francis W. O'Brien.

353. Joseph Missley letter contained in O'Brien NJSP Museum file.

354. Dr. George N.J. Sommer to Dr. Haggerty, January 29, 1941; Captain W.J. Carter to Colonel Chas. H Schoeffel, April 21, 1939; Samuel B. English, MD, to Major Mark O. Kimberling, April 27, 1939; Major Mark O. Kimberling to Samuel B. English, MD, April 28, 1939; Samuel B. English, MD, to Major Mark O. Kimberling, April 29, 1939; Samuel B. English, MD, to Dr. S.T. Day, March 3, 1942; Dr. George N.J. Sommer to Dr. Haggerty, January 29, 1941; Dr. George N.J. Sommer to Dr. Haggerty, January 20, 1941; Joseph Missley letter.

355. Ibid.

356. Interview with Francis W. O'Brien.

357. Ibid.

358. Ibid.

AXE KILLING AND THE SHOOTING OF A TROOPER

359. Abe J. Green to Colonel H. Norman Schwarzkopf, July 25, 1934; Reverend Philip McCool to Colonel Schwarzkopf, July 30, 1934.

360. NJSP Special Order #8, July 17, 1945.

361. Interview with Monsignor O'Donnell.

362. Ibid.

363. NJSP Special Order #8, July 17, 1945.

364. Abe J. Green to Colonel H. Norman Schwarzkopf, July 25, 1934.

365. Cornelius A. O'Donnell NJSP Museum file.

366. Interview with Monsignor O'Donnell.

367. *Newark Evening News*, July 16, 1945.

368. Ibid.

369. Ibid.

370. Ibid.

371. Ibid.

372. Ibid.

373. Ibid.

374. Ibid.

375. NJSP Special Order #8, July 17, 1945; interview with Monsignor O'Donnell.

376. NJSP Special Order #8, July 17, 1945.

EXCESSIVE SPEED

377. NJSP Personnel Order #299, September 27, 1948; ePodunk, "Egg Harbor, New Jersey," http://www.epodunk.com/cgi-bin/genInfo.php?locIndex=18018; Wikipedia, "Egg Harbor, New Jersey," http://en.wikipedia.org/wiki/Egg_Harbor_Township,_New_Jersey.

378. NJSP Personnel Order #299, September 27, 1948; untitled NJSP document, September 27, 1948.

379. "Atlantic City, New Jersey," www.Atlanticcity.com; NJSP Personnel Order #299, September 27, 1948.

380. New Jersey State Police Personnel Order Number 299, dated September 27, 1948.

381. Ibid.

382. *Farmer's Almanac*, http://www.almanac.com/weatherhistory/; NJSP Personnel Order #299, September 27, 1948; NJSP official website, www.njsp.org.

383. NJSP Personnel Order #299, September 27, 1948; untitled NJSP document, September 27, 1948.

384. NJSP accident report, September 27, 1948.

385. NJSP Personnel Order #299, September 27, 1948.

386. Ibid.

STOP SIGN

387. NJSP Personnel Order #68, April 22, 1950; Wikipedia, "Garfield, New Jersey," http://en.wikipedia.org/wiki/Garfield,_NJ; interview with Walter Gawryla (nephew), August 18, 2008.

388. Kingwood College Library, "American Cultural History, 1920–1929," http://kclibrary.lonestar.edu/decade20.html; Wikipedia, "Roaring Twenties," http://en.wikipedia.org/wiki/Roaring_twenties; interview with Walter Gawryla, August 18, 2008; Walter Gawryla to John O'Rourke, July 26, 2008.

389. NJSP Personnel Order #68, April 22, 1950.

390. Ibid.; interview with Walter Gawryla, August 18, 2008; Walter Gawryla to John O'Rourke, July 26, 2008.

391. NJSP Personnel Order #68, April 22, 1950.

392. Ibid.

393. Interview with Walter Gawryla, August 18, 2008; Walter Gawryla to John O'Rourke, July 26, 2008; NJSP Personnel Order #127, December 10, 1947; *Farmer's Almanac*, http://www.almanac.com/weatherhistory/.

394. NJSP Personnel Order #299, September 27, 1948.

395. NJSP official website, www.njsp.org.

396. *Farmer's Almanac*, http://www.almanac.com/weatherhistory; *Hunterdon County Democrat*, April 22, 1950; interview with Walter Gawryla, August 18, 2008; Walter Gawryla to John O'Rourke, July 26, 2008.

FATE

397. NJSP Personnel Order #83, May 28, 1951; NJSP official website, www.njsp.org; Coakley, *Jersey Troopers*; Wikipedia, "Roaring Twenties," http://en.wikipedia.org/wiki/Roaring_twenties.

398. House of Names, www.houseofnames.com; Behind the Name, http://surnames.behindthename.com; NJSP Personnel Order #83, May 28, 1951; State Department of Health of New Jersey Death Certificate of Emil Bock, May 26, 1951.

399. NJSP Personnel Order #83, May 28, 1951; State Department of Health of New Jersey Death Certificate of Emil Bock, May 26, 1951.

400. NJSP Personnel Order #83, May 28, 1951.

401. "American Cultural History," http://kclibrary.lonestar.edu/decade50.html; Fifties Web, www.fifitiesweb.com.

402. NJSP Personnel Order #189, December 18, 1950.

403. Coakley, *Jersey Troopers*.

404. Emil J. Bock to Captain H.A. Carlson, April 20, 1951; NJSP Personnel Order #83, May 28, 1951.

405. NJSP preliminary report, May 26, 1951.

406. Ibid.

407. NJSP Personnel Order #83, May 28, 1951.

KICKSTAND

408. Interview with James Conn (brother).

409. NJSP Personnel Order #131, August 28, 1951; interview with James Conn.

410. Ibid.

411. Interview with James Conn; Stanley A. Conn Jr. NJSP Museum file.

412. Ibid.

413. Ibid.

414. Ibid.

415. Ibid.

416. *Paterson Evening News*, August 28, 1951, and August 29, 1951.

417. NJSP Personnel Order #131, August 28, 1951.

STRANGE

418. James D. Wirth NJSP Museum file; Interview with James Wirth and Margarete Wirth.

419. Ibid.

420. Ibid.

421. Interview with James Wirth and Margarete Wirth; Wikipedia, "USS Mississippi," http://en.wikipedia.org/wiki/USS_Mississippi_%28BB-41%29.

422. Interview with James Wirth and Margarete Wirth.

423. NJSP official website, www.njsp.org; *Farmer's Almanac*, http://www.almanac.com/weatherhistory; interview with James Wirth and Margarete Wirth.

424. Interview with James Wirth and Margarete Wirth; Lieutenant J. Wolf to Captain D.J. Dunn, December 6, 1951; Hudson County Boulevard Police Department report of arrest, November 25, 1951, authored by Lieutenant Herlihy; Bayonne Police Department Accident Report, November 25, 1951; memorandum to attorney general, August 5, 1952.

425. Ibid.

426. Ibid.

427. Lieutenant J. Wolf to Captain D.J. Dunn, November 28, 1951.

OVERTURN

428. Interview with Patricia and Eileen, February 13, 2008.

429. Ibid.

430. Ibid.

431. New Jersey State Police Special Order #666, November 14, 1938.

432. Interview with Patricia and Eileen Walter, February 13, 2008.

433. Ibid.

434. Ibid.

435. Russell A. Snook, undated and unnumbered Special Order; interview with Patricia and Eileen Walter, February 13, 2008.

436. Interview with Patricia and Eileen Walter, February 13, 2008.

437. Ibid.

438. NJSP teletype, August 14, 1952; NJSP teletype, September 7, 1952.

439. Ibid.; interview with Patricia and Eileen Walter, February 13, 2008.

440. NJSP teletype, August 14, 1952; NJSP teletype, September 7, 1952.

441. NJSP Personnel Order #170, September 8, 1952.

NEW JERSEY TURNPIKE

442. Frank A. Trainor NJSP Museum file.

443. www.surnames.com; "McCabe Clan," www.mccabeclan.com.

444. New Jersey Turnpike Authority Accident Report, August 3, 1953; Trainor NJSP Museum file.

445. New Jersey Turnpike Authority Accident Report, August 3, 1953.

446. Ibid.

447. Trainor NJSP Museum file.

ROBBERY, MURDER AND THE TAKING OF A HOSTAGE ON ROUTE 66

448. Interview with Helen Hartwiger; NJSP Personnel Order #132, November 3, 1955.
449. Interview with Helen Hartwiger.
450. Ibid.
451. Ibid.
452. Ibid.
453. Ibid.; NJSP Personnel Order #132, November 3, 1955.
454. "History of Route 66," http://www.national66.org/66hstry.html; Wikipedia, "U.S. Route 66," http://en.wikipedia.org/wiki/U.S._Route_66.
455. *Daily Record*, November 4, 1955; *Newark Evening News*, November 2, 1955; unknown newspaper article clippings contained in John Anderson NJSP Museum file; *Brown v. Board of Education*, 347 U.S. 483 (1954).
456. Ibid.
457. Ibid.
458. Ibid.
459. Ibid.
460. Ibid.
461. Ibid.
462. Ibid.
463. Ibid.
464. Ibid.
465. Interview with Helen Hartwiger; "Autumn Leaves," written by Johnny Mercer.

"FIGHT IN PROGRESS"

466. NJSP Personnel Order #44, May 29, 1956; interview with Barbara Dancy Hubscher, March 31, 2007.
467. "The Presidents of the United States," http://www.whitehouse.gov/history/presidents; interview with Barbara Dancy Hubscher.
468. Interview with David Dancy.
469. Interview with Barbara Dancy Hubscher.
470. Ibid.
471. Ibid.
472. Interview with Barbara Dancy Hubscher; interview with David Dancy.
473. Ibid.
474. Ibid.
475. Interview with Barbara Dancy Hubscher.
476. NJSP Special Order #44, May 29, 1956; interview with Barbara Dancy Hubscher.
477. Interview with Barbara Dancy Hubscher.
478. Ibid.
479. Author's personal knowledge and opinion.
480. Interview with Barbara Dancy Hubscher.
481. Interview with David Dancy.
482. Interview with Carol Huscher Cirillo.
483. Interview with David Dancy.

COURT

484. Finley Fuchs NJSP Museum file; NJSP untitled and dated report signed by Finley Fuchs; House of Names, www.houseofnames.com.

485. Ibid.

486. NJSP Special Order #111, August 16, 1955; *Farmer's Almanac*, http://www.almanac.com/weatherhistory.

487. Fuchs NJSP Museum file; NJSP untitled and dated report signed by Finley Fuchs.

488. NJSP accident report by Sergeant.McLaughlin #890, December 19, 1957; Detective G.C. Dollar to Captain D.C. Borchard, January 2, 1958; Fuchs NJSP Museum file.

489. Detective G.C. Dollar to Captain D.C. Borchard, January 2, 1958; Fuchs NJSP Museum file.

490. Ibid.

491. Ibid.

492. Ibid.

493. Ibid.

MYSTERY

494. Ronald Gray NJSP Museum file; NJSP Personnel Order #123, December 2, 1958; Wikipedia, "Rutherford, New Jersey," http://en.wikipedia.org/wiki/Rutherford,_NJ; ePodunk, "Rutherford, New Jersey," http://www.epodunk.com/cgi-bin/genInfo.php?locIndex=18600; "The Great Depression," http://www.english.illinois.edu/maps/depression/depression.htm.

495. Unnamed newspaper article of accident, December 1, 1958; Gray NJSP Museum file.

496. NJSP Personnel Order #123, December 2, 1958; Wikipedia, "Rutherford, New Jersey," http://en.wikipedia.org/wiki/Rutherford,_NJ; ePodunk, "Rutherford, New Jersey," http://www.epodunk.com/cgi-bin/genInfo.php?locIndex=18600.

497. NJSP Personnel Order #123, December 2, 1958; NJSP official website, www.njsp.org.

498. Gray NJSP Museum file; unnamed newspaper article of accident, December 1, 1958.

499. Family members declined interview.

500. Author's own knowledge.

501. Unnamed newspaper article of accident, December 1, 1958; Gray NJSP Museum file.

502. NJSP Personnel Order #123, December 2, 1958.

503. Deputy Attorney General Charles I. Levine to Felix Bigotto, September 24, 1959.

MOTORIST AID

504. "History of Burlington, New Jersey," http://www.twp.burlington.nj.us.

505. Sandra Pennepede to John O'Rourke, February 22, 2010; interview with Mary Ann Yuengling.

506. Ibid.

507. Ibid.

508. Ibid.

509. Ibid.

510. Ibid.

511. Ibid.

512. Ibid.

513. Ibid.

514. Ibid.

515. Captain J.A. Wolf to Colonel J.D. Rutter, superintendent, November 17, 1955; *Farmer's Almanac*, http://www.almanac.com/weatherhistory.

516. Ibid.

517. Sandy Pennepede to John O'Rourke, March 2, 2010.

518. NJSP teletype #785 File 3, November 20, 1959; NJSP document of Frederick Cidone's statements, n.d.; NJSP operations report, November 20, 1959.

519. Ibid.

520. Interview with Mary Ann Yuengling.

521. NJSP teletype #785 File 3, November 20, 1959; Sandra Pennepede to John O'Rourke, February 22, 2010; interview with Mary Ann Yuengling.

ABOUT THE AUTHOR

J ohn E. O'Rourke was born in Pequannock, New Jersey, and raised in
the Passaic County town of Wanaque. O'Rourke's education includes a
bachelor of science degree from Thomas Edison State College and a master
of arts degree from Seton Hall University. He has an extensive background in
police and security leadership and is board certified in security management
from the American Society for Industrial Security, International (ASIS).
Presently, O'Rourke is the chair of the Crime and Loss Prevention Council
for ASIS and is a twenty-five-year veteran with the New Jersey State Police.
He is stationed at Troop E Headquarters in Holmdel, New Jersey.

Visit us at
www.historypress.net